AF798025

JONATHAN VAN VIEGEN

CHOOSING US

STORIES AND STRATEGIES TO STRENGTHEN YOUR MARRIAGE FROM INSIDE THE THERAPY ROOM

JOSSEY-BASS™
A Wiley Brand

Copyright © 2027 by John Wiley & Sons, Inc. All rights reserved, including rights for text and data mining and training of artificial intelligence technologies or similar technologies.

Published by John Wiley & Sons, Inc., Hoboken, New Jersey.

No part of this publication may be reproduced, stored in a retrieval system, or transmitted in any form or by any means, electronic, mechanical, photocopying, recording, scanning, or otherwise, except as permitted under Section 107 or 108 of the 1976 United States Copyright Act, without either the prior written permission of the Publisher, or authorization through payment of the appropriate per-copy fee to the Copyright Clearance Center, Inc., 222 Rosewood Drive, Danvers, MA 01923, (978) 750-8400, fax (978) 750-4470, or on the web at www.copyright.com. Requests to the Publisher for permission should be addressed to the Permissions Department, John Wiley & Sons, Inc., 111 River Street, Hoboken, NJ 07030, (201) 748-6011, fax (201) 748-6008, or online at http://www.wiley.com/go/permission.

The manufacturer's authorized representative according to the EU General Product Safety Regulation is Wiley-VCH GmbH, Boschstr. 12, 69469 Weinheim, Germany, e-mail: Product_Safety@wiley.com.

Trademarks: Wiley and the Wiley logo are trademarks or registered trademarks of John Wiley & Sons, Inc. and/or its affiliates in the United States and other countries and may not be used without written permission. All other trademarks are the property of their respective owners. John Wiley & Sons, Inc. is not associated with any product or vendor mentioned in this book.

Limit of Liability/Disclaimer of Warranty: While the publisher and the authors have used their best efforts in preparing this work, including a review of the content of the work, neither the publisher nor the authors make any representations or warranties with respect to the accuracy or completeness of the contents of this work and specifically disclaim all warranties, including without limitation any implied warranties of merchantability or fitness for a particular purpose. No warranty may be created or extended by sales representatives, written sales materials or promotional statements for this work. The fact that an organization, website, or product is referred to in this work as a citation and/or potential source of further information does not mean that the publisher and authors endorse the information or services the organization, website, or product may provide or recommendations it may make. This work is sold with the understanding that the publisher is not engaged in rendering professional services. The advice and strategies contained herein may not be suitable for your situation. You should consult with a specialist where appropriate. Further, readers should be aware that websites listed in this work may have changed or disappeared between when this work was written and when it is read. Neither the publisher nor authors shall be liable for any loss of profit or any other commercial damages, including but not limited to special, incidental, consequential, or other damages.

For general information on our other products and services or for technical support, please contact our Customer Care Department within the United States at (800) 762-2974, outside the United States at (317) 572-3993 or fax (317) 572-4002.

Wiley also publishes its books in a variety of electronic formats. Some content that appears in print may not be available in electronic formats. For more information about Wiley products, visit our web site at www.wiley.com.

Library of Congress Cataloging-in-Publication Data has been applied for:

ISBN 9781394387014 (Hardback)
ISBN 9781394387021 (ePub)
ISBN 9781394387038 (ePDF)

Cover Design: Wiley
Author Photo: José Castillo

Printed and bound by CPI Group (UK) Ltd, Croydon, CR0 4YY

C9781394387014_100926

For my wife,
Meredith
— For choosing me.

And my daughters,
Charlotte and Aria
— So they know what it means to be cherished.

Contents

Prologue: To Be Chosen and Cherished...or Not

The other day, I was talking with my wife, and it occurred to me that I had never once in my life seen my parents kiss. Or hug. Let alone repair after a fight. That's because they divorced when I was four years old. The impact of that? I never witnessed, firsthand, what a healthy marital relationship looks like.

Instead of being taught about connection, I was brainwashed. By my own father, nonetheless.

He taught me not to trust women. Yet he was the one who was unfaithful. He taught me women were out to get men. To manipulate men. To him, women were conniving and underhanded, yet he was the one legally on the hook for tens of thousands of dollars of child support he owed to my mother. And when she wouldn't agree to cancel the debt he owed her, he kidnapped my sister and me. We didn't see our mother for three months.

That was the abusive and toxic role model I had growing up.

Needless to say, my expectations of women—and marriage—were low.

Sadly, I believed all the lies my father told me about women. It wasn't until I turned 32 that I decided the pain of loneliness was greater than learning to trust one.

That's when I met Meredith.

That's when panic hit.

And that's when I needed a book like this the most.

If you find yourself in similar shoes—panic hijacking your nervous system like it did mine, or pain making you wonder if there's anything good left—then you're exactly who I wrote this book for.

Now is not the time to ask yourself if it's too late. Save that for another day. Today is about giving you the tools to do more than just save your marriage. Today is when you learn how to make it feel chosen and cherished.

Back to My Whirlwind Romance...

By the end of our first date, I knew Meredith checked all my boxes. Physically she was my type. She was smart and funny, and her extrovert balanced out my introvert perfectly.

By the end of our second date, I knew I had all the pieces I needed to satisfy the emotional connection I craved. I got home from eating sushi, called my mother and sister, and told them I'd met my future wife. Three months later, I asked her to marry me.

Exactly 10 months after our first date, we were married. Our wedding was beautiful. Like Cinderella, everything was perfect—until midnight.

That's when all the years of anxiety bubbled to the surface and convinced me that the woman I'd just married wasn't the woman I thought she was, all because she danced a little too close to one of our wedding guests. In an instant, I saw the threat my father warned me about and decided she was going to break my heart.

Telling you that story, something I've not shared publicly once in 17 years, brings me more than therapeutic release. It allows me to share the lesson I learned about not giving up. That's the lesson my mother taught me. Perseverance is the single most important ingredient for turning tragedy into triumph.

My mother didn't just teach me. She showed me.

She taught me that unless you find yourself married to a man who makes you so afraid that you leave a set of car keys hidden outside in the event you have to run for your life, you don't give up on your relationship.

My mother did run on her last night with my father and had to leave us kids behind.

I don't know his name, but I'd like to thank the sheriff who escorted her back three days later to take us home.

But I digress.

Perseverance, that's what I'm talking about. And it's the first message I want to speak to you about. I've spent 18 years fighting back at the anxiety I feel, knowing I can be hurt by the one woman I love more than anything. Were there weeks, months, or even years in my relationship that I thought I was going to fail?

Absolutely.

I'd go so far as to say that, for the first six years of my marriage, I didn't think we'd make it. But I never gave up. I refused to quit on my wife and, thankfully, she refused to quit on me.

The reality is that people just aren't that good at predicting how they'll feel about their spouse in the future. Case in point, I've no idea if in five years I'll still want to live in Central America. I may wake up and decide it's time to move.

The same is true for relationships. The spouse you're not "in love" with today may be the spouse you fall back in love with next week, next month, or next year. That's why relying on your feelings will sell you short. But relying on perseverance? That's what pays off.

That's why I don't tell people, "I save marriages." I sell them on the idea that they can save their own.

I Don't Save Marriages

As therapists, we don't save people's marriages. Sure, many of us think that's what we do. But we don't. At least, no couples therapist that I know does. The reality is that we're in the business of changing people's minds.

And that's what this book is about: three couples who resisted the idea that changing how they think about their marriage could save it—until changing their minds saved it.

I used to think I was terrible at convincing people. Still do, really. It just doesn't come naturally to me. And to be honest, it's not something I've ever cared all that much about.

Meredith on the other hand? She can sell anything. Me? I can barely get people to subscribe to my email list.

To me, selling has always felt like trying to convince people of something they didn't know they wanted. Until it comes to marriages. That's where I come alive. That's where I shine. And that's what I was put on this earth to do.

Thinking back to the first time I sat with a couple, I must have looked like an eight-year-old in Willy Wonka's chocolate factory, waving around my master's degree like a golden ticket. The moment I sat down, I was hooked. And I haven't looked back since.

Every new couple that comes to me is more than a case. The second they say something like, "We really don't like each other," that's when I jump into action. Even before they tell me their names, I'm scanning. Like an F1 driver, I'm taking it all in and processing a million things a minute. How they're sitting next to each other. Their tone. Their outfits. Even their lighting. Is it natural? Artificial? And are they trying to blind me by sitting in front of a window?

Why is all this important? Because it tells a story. Their story. And I dig until I know everything about them there is to know. I want to know what kind of marriage they're living in, because the stakes are high. Enormously high.

By the time most couples come to me, they are playing high-stakes poker with their marriage. They don't know which way to place their bet, and they look to me to help them decide. The pressure on me is real. But that's exactly how I like it.

Every couple you're about to read about felt deep emotional pain at the thought of impending divorce. And they wanted nothing more than to avoid it like the plague—for themselves and their children. And that's why I do this job. I hate divorce. I've lived through my parents'—twice over for both—and will gladly square off against it any day of the week. Every couple has it in them to turn things around and go in the opposite direction. But only if they believe they can.

And That's Where I Come In

What I do along the way is ask a few questions, share a few tools, and introduce all the strategies I use in self-preservation to keep my own marriage intact after 17 years. It's a fine line I have to walk with my clients. If I confuse them, I lose them. Or make things worse.

My job is to get my clients to believe they have what it takes to save their marriage. If I fail, it's more than their money back that they deserve. It's a pound of my flesh. That's the pressure I put on myself.

Thankfully, I succeed from time to time.

This book will show you how to do the same.

You're going to get a behind-the-scenes peek at how I did exactly that with three couples: one struggling with betrayal, one struggling with conflict, and one fighting back against years of emotional decay.

This book, and the journey I'm going to take you on, is going to be really simple. Because simple is the best way to learn.

That doesn't mean the methods I teach are easy to master. But if you read English at a grade 5 level, you'll be just fine. There's very little psycho-babble or therapist jargon to confuse you.

You'll discover I don't play the diagnosing game. And I don't use attachment theory or love languages in my work. This is not because they aren't helpful, but I believe they oversimplify what's going on in a relationship by focusing on only half the story: the painful half.

In most relationships, you'll find more joy than pain—if you dare to look for it. That's why couples need language that helps them find it. And that's exactly what this book gives you. I don't believe that relationships require a better expression of "needs" to be healthy. In fact, I believe it's the opposite. And later in this book, you'll understand why.

Most of what the "experts" talk about today is far too complicated. And for the average person, it just creates confusion. Talking about your feelings ad nauseam leads to overthinking. And that rarely transforms a marriage. If anything, it teaches you to prioritize self-soothing over self-sacrifice, and it drives couples further apart. If there was no need to psychoanalyze the honeymoon phase of your relationship, there's no need to do it now.

Couples need something far simpler. They need mindfulness—but not the Deepak Chopra or Joe Dispenza kind. I'm talking about being mindful of the language you use, down to the words you choose.

You're going to learn how to correct your messaging. If your messaging is off, your marriage will be, too. It's that simple. By the time you finish this book, you'll know exactly how to send the one message worth focusing on. You'll be so mindful of it, it becomes automatic. That is how you're going to save your marriage.

The only message worth communicating to your partner—on the daily—is this:

You are chosen. And you are cherished.

If you want to write that down, now would be a good time. You could even go so far as to tattoo it on your forearm.

Here's What You Need to Know to Get the Most Out of This Book

For each couple, I'm going to take you through five sessions, starting with the crisis and ending with hope. You'll read their stories, follow our conversations, and see exactly how I guide them in saving their marriage.

Each chapter is filled with the interventions I use to help these three couples. They include questions I use every day in my practice. I've italicized the questions to make them easy for you to identify and refer back to. They apply to almost all relationships and can easily be adjusted to suit yours.

At the end of each chapter, I'll pause and give you a few important takeaways I want you to remember.

If you're worried, yes, you can absolutely do this work on your own. I know, because I did. Sure, Meredith came along for the ride. But even if she hadn't—or was reluctant—this still works when one partner commits to it.

It's likely your situation won't match the couples in this book exactly. That doesn't matter. You'll learn how to apply these principles in your own relationship.

All of the characters in this book are fictitious and completely made up by me. Any resemblance to real-life people is completely coincidental.

I use words like *marriage* and *relationship* interchangeably throughout this book. As I do spouse and partner. Don't get hung up on my word choice. This isn't just for married couples. It's for any two committed people who want their relationship to work.

Finally, I want to leave you with this: couples work should feel good. There is nothing about the work I do with couples that is meant to hurt. If that is the case, please put the book down. People don't improve under stress. Connecting you with your pain—like many of my peers prefer to do—is not what I believe you need if your intended purpose is to repair your relationship.

Couples don't need more of what they don't want—heartache. They need faith. Faith in themselves. Faith in each other. Faith in their relationship. If I can help you find that, then I've done my job.

I've been doing this work for more than a decade, so a lot of this comes automatically to me. It won't for you—at least not right away. But don't worry about that.

You don't need perfection. You just need progress.

—In solutions and strength,
Jonathan

Part I

Vanessa and Julian: Surviving Infidelity

Chapter 1

Don't Ask Why (What Comes First After Betrayal)

The twins had just turned 11 months old when Vanessa found the piece of paper that brought her world crashing down.

She and Julian had decided she'd stay home indefinitely with the girls. She'd never imagined being anything but a lawyer. But the moment she laid eyes on them, she knew that leaving them to sit in an office all day was something she'd never be able to do. Julian's job in private equity provided more than enough. The beach house wasn't going anywhere, even without her salary.

She'd planned to hit Send that morning on the email telling her boss she wasn't coming back when her maternity leave ended. She'd written it a week ago, but couldn't bring herself to send it. Something made her wait.

After getting the girls down for their morning nap, another load of laundry prolonged her procrastination.

Checking his pockets like she always did, Vanessa found the prescription. In an instant, she felt her heart sink. What in the world did he need an antibiotic for? He'd woken up feeling fine, even said he was going to stop at the gym on his way home. How was doxycycline making an appearance in his morning routine? The rest of the day passed in a blur of worry, confusion, and a deep-down dread.

After dinner, when he got home and the girls were finally asleep, she found out. Before he confessed to everything, Julian first gave her the runaround. At least he tried. Vanessa was a seasoned litigator, often first chair on the firm's biggest cases. Julian couldn't have hidden the truth even if he wanted to. That's how they ended up in my calendar six days later.

"Were you showing any symptoms?" I asked Julian.

"No. I just knew I screwed up badly. But I just wanted to protect her."

That didn't feel like protection, I thought. I'll be candid for a second. Infidelity has always been a trigger for me. It still tests my professionalism to this day. The truth is that I can't get the image out of my mind of my 30-something mother with two kids at home sitting in her car in a run-down motel parking lot in Buffalo at 11 p.m. watching my dad slink inside with two big-haired prostitutes.

Stories like the one I'm about to share with you simply hit too close to home; my heart can't help but ache for the young mother sitting in front of me. After 10 years in this field, I've had more than my fill of exposure to infidelity. Certainly enough to know how incredibly painful yet unmistakably human it is. I'm also keenly aware of how easily it stirs up my own childhood.

I scribble a small reminder in my session notes to bring this reaction up in supervision. My supervisor, Susan, won't hold back on me when I do. She keeps me grounded and practicing ethically. She'll happily hold a mirror up to me while taking another bite of her chicken burrito bowl.

Susan is opinionated, often profane, and quick to call me out if she catches even a whiff of me over-identifying with a client. And I like that. For the better part of a decade, she's been a constant force behind my commitment to clinical excellence. I owe a huge part of my integrity as a practitioner to her, far more than she'd allow me to credit.

But for now, back to Julian. He was at an energy conference in Vegas when it happened. After a long day of pressing hands with venture capitalists and regulators, he was starving. He took a taxi back to his room at the Hilton, grabbed a quick shower, and instead of raiding the mini-bar, headed downstairs for a scotch and a steak. That's where he met her.

Sometime between his third and fourth refill, an attractive woman approached him. Whether it was the alcohol, fatigue, the first taste of freedom since becoming a father, or all three, we'll never know. What matters is that he took her back to his room.

God help us, I thought. What do they put in the water in Vegas that makes people forget they're married? This was the second client in six months who'd cheated on a work trip there.

But sitting there beside his wife, head hanging low, you couldn't help but feel bad for the guy. He had everything any man could ever ask for. And here he was, fighting for his life.

If I could, I'd love nothing better than to run the clock back for him. Tap his shoulder at the bar and tell him to go to bed. Or better yet, tell him that I had a story to share with him. A story about a guy who'd spend the next decade trying to live down 30 minutes in a Vegas hotel room. A guy who risked everything for a moment that would never come close to what it cost him in the end.

But that's not what happened. In the end, Julian came clean. It took him an hour to wake up from his self-inflicted nightmare. And when he did, he told her everything.

When the initial tears had abated, and numbness was setting in, Julian made quick work and found me. First he left a voicemail. When I didn't return his call within the hour, he followed up with an email. At that moment, I'd had neither the time nor enough caffeine in my system to reply to him.

But an hour later, while finishing a reel for Instagram, I saw his DM come in. I knew instantly that there was a live one on the hook.

"Hi Julian, you're really trying to reach me," I messaged him.

"Yes, thanks for getting back to me," he replied. "I tried your voicemail and email."

"I saw that. Apologies for not replying earlier. Let me call you now."

"That would be great, thank you."

I punched in his phone number, and I don't think it rang twice.

"Hi, Jonathan," he said quickly. "Thanks for calling."

"Of course," I reassured him. "Tell me, what's going on?"

"I pulled the rug out from under her," he said. "I cheated on my wife."

At least he had the wherewithal to recognize that, I thought.

Julian spent the next 10 minutes telling me what had happened. "I'm so pathetic. I need help. Please help me," he wrapped up with.

And listen, just because Julian's had a coming-to-Jesus moment doesn't mean the process of repair has started. He's not even close. His wife is carrying way too much pain for anyone to even say the word *repair* right now. We're still in the stop-the-bleeding phase.

But for all his panic, it was clear from our first call that Julian wasn't new to crisis. Business school teaches you how to perform under pressure. And if it doesn't, the 80-hour weeks most young analysts spend in the meat grinder will.

That's what investment banking does to you. It trains you to think decisively and move fast. "The best offense is a good defense" is how he put it. You didn't need to be clairvoyant to understand that hesitation wasn't going to end well for him.

Vanessa wouldn't disappear quietly if their marriage ended in divorce, he told me. She was too smart for that. Too good of an attorney for that. Plus, she had award-winning, jugular-sniffing lawyer friends on speed dial.

But that wasn't the real reason he wanted my help. He loved her. He loved the girls. He loved their life. He wasn't ready to let it come to an end. And he wanted to save it. Julian shifted again in his seat, and my mind was pulled back into our first session.

"How did I screw this up?" he wondered, as if he didn't know.

You paid for sex with a woman you met in a hotel bar while your wife was home with your twin girls, I almost let slip.

"You lost your moral compass," I replied instead. "That doesn't mean it's gone forever. Or that there wasn't one there in the first place."

He looked at me, confused.

"Do you mind if we go in a different direction for a moment?" I continued. "How you got into this mess isn't important right now."

"How so?" he asked as if mocking me.

"Look. Right now, we've got bigger issues than trying to figure out why you stepped outside of your marriage," I said. "We need a path forward out of this mess. And we're about to find out if you two have enough faith in yourselves to walk it."

He gave me that look again—confused, disappointed. The kind I imagined he gave his underlings. He didn't like not understanding his own decisions.

"Look at her," I said, leaving no room for negotiation.

He turned and did.

"If that's my wife, her tears are going to bother me. She's in a lot of pain. We need to triage that, now. Because if we don't, her flame will go out. And she'll leave to light it somewhere else."

Julian's confusion was gone.

"So, allow me to jump in with a little advice," I continued. "I strongly suggest we stop asking 'why' this all happened so we can pack this wound before we all bleed out in this office."

Now, I'm going to pause Vanessa's and Julian's story for a New York minute. I need to explain why we don't ask "why" in therapy.

As therapists, we're trained to help, not to gossip. This isn't the Bored Housewives of WhatsApp. We focus on what actually moves our clients forward. And asking why someone did something? It doesn't.

If your marriage is in crisis, then replaying the details won't make you feel better. That doesn't mean the truth should be ignored. It needs to come out. But the details of *what* happened are different from *why* it happened.

Here's why dissecting the "why" isn't helpful. First, the why is "unknowable." And it changes constantly. To prove my point, ask yourself why you said yes to your spouse today versus on your wedding day, and you'll arrive at two different answers.

That's because humans forget things. Our memories are faulty. And our stories change. So if the answer can change with time, then the question isn't useful.

Second, it can't move you forward. If anything, it keeps you stuck in the past. Knowing why it rains doesn't prevent you from getting rained on. And if your marriage is in a crisis, you're getting wet. So, you have a choice to make: ask mother nature why it's raining, or grab an umbrella when you leave the house.

Third, and this is what's lost on most people: connecting someone to how they screwed up their marriage is the single fastest way to stall the healing process.

Take Julian. If I anchor him in shame, not only will he feel defeated and hopeless, he'll struggle hard to find any confidence that he can change. Couples struggling in intense emotional pain don't need change three months from now. They need change now.

Getting to the root cause of anything isn't going to make the tears abate any faster. One look at Vanessa and you can see she's barely holding on. Her husband had unprotected sex in a Vegas hotel room and needed a prescription because of it. Wrap your head around that.

You think she has months of "processing" in her? She doesn't.

That's not what I do anyway.

I help couples change now. I'm taking Vanessa and Julian where they actually want to go: back to honesty, fidelity, loyalty…and hope. If I don't give them an off-ramp to the pain, they'll never find it themselves. And to his credit, Julian didn't wait long to take it.

"Is it okay for me to question who I am?" he asked.

"Of course it is. Every man would if he were in your shoes," I answered. "It's not every day that you hurt someone you love so deeply."

"That's what I can't get out of my head. All the pain I caused her. All the shame I brought on me. On us," he said sheepishly. "I hate myself for shattering our identity."

"You should hate yourself!" Vanessa snapped. "I gave everything to you, and apparently it still wasn't good enough. How am I supposed to trust you after what you did to me? How am I ever supposed to believe I'm enough for you?"

Ooh, that one hurt, I thought.

All of a sudden her composure changed. Gone was the anger on her face. It was replaced by the look only a lost child could give.

"I'm scared to leave. But I'm more scared to stay," she said to me, as if I had the answer.

And that's when the bombshell about almost leaving her job made sense to me. The stakes were high. Does she forgive her husband and keep her career on hold? Or does she leave now, find a nanny, and go back to work? If we can't repair this and their marriage fails, what then?

"Is this fixable?" she asked.

I couldn't have timed it better if I was Hans Zimmer scoring *The Lion King* when they both turned their heads and looked directly at me.

"Of course this is fixable. And let me tell you how...," I said, without a trace of doubt.

Before I tell you what I said, I have to tell you what I didn't. Because what's left unspoken is more powerful than what is.

When Julian left his first voicemail, he didn't lead with what he'd done. In fact, he downplayed it.

"We're having some trust issues," he said.

Trust issues, eh? That's not how I'd have framed it. Sarcasm aside, there's a reason why he didn't lead with his shame. He didn't trust me. Because he didn't know me. Sure, he watched my videos on Instagram. Liked what he saw. But that's not trust.

Vanessa, on the other hand, is so hurt right now that she'll trust anyone but Julian. And this moment—the First Touch, as I call it—is make or break for us.

They're coming to me from wildly different places. Vanessa trusts me, but not him. Julian trusts Vanessa, not me. What I do next is super-critical. I have to be the steady hand—not the corrupt politician kind but the one they can trust. If they don't trust me, and this process, I will fail.

So no, they're not here to "work on trust." That would be whitewashing it. He got drunk and slept with a prostitute. That's the reason they're here. And that's where we start.

Despite my distaste for what Julian did, I haven't written him off—not by a long shot. I choose to see the good in him. In everyone, actually. And if that sounds naive to you, you need to understand that it's not. It's critical, in fact. If I can't show Vanessa that I see the man beneath his mistake, neither will she.

When I look at you, I don't see the mustard on your shirt. I'm too busy wiping the ketchup off mine. Now, don't get me wrong: I call out behavior, Julian's included. But judging it isn't my job. My faith says that is God's.

When I see someone hunched over on a street corner, I don't choose to see a junkie with a needle sticking out of his arm. I see a brother, son, friend, or neighbor. For me, I see the beautiful person underneath their choices.

And so, from the second I met Julian face-to-face, I wanted him to know that I'm not here to be his judge, jury, and executioner. I know he's a good man, a good husband, a good father. Just one who made a gravely poor decision.

I tell him that I've seen this before. I've got this, and we'll get through this. I know he feels like what he's done is worthy of sending him to Hell. But am I the one to put him there? Absolutely not. I'm here to help him feel whole again.

"Julian? Whole again? WTAF? What about Vanessa?!!" I can hear you shouting.

Slow down. Don't burn this book quite yet. I'm not going to let you run off believing I'm a second-rate therapist. I've got the image of twin 11-month-old girls in my head, and I can't stop thinking: What about the kids?

Their future—growing up in an intact family or not—hangs over my head. That's got a lot to do with what my sister and I lived through. So yes, my focus is on them. On keeping their parents together.

And the biggest long-term threat to that isn't what Vanessa thinks of Julian. It's what Julian thinks of himself. Before you cancel me, I didn't say short-term. I'm talking long-term. And before you accuse me of going easy on Julian, I'm not giving him a pass for what he did.

But there is a duality in every relationship that most people fail to recognize. You can love someone and hate what they did. Hate them even. Both things can be true, as they are for Vanessa. She loves him. Is devastated by him. And still wants to stay with him.

What I think of him is irrelevant. They came to me with a broken relationship. Not the one you'd post on Instagram. They're the messy, conflicted, falling-apart kind. But if they're willing to fight for it, then it's my job to show them how.

Coming back to the short-term: Vanessa is going to have to forgive him enough to like him. Then like him enough to want to love him again. Of course, that's easier said than done. But that's what I do all day, every day with couples.

The hard part is going to be piecing Julian's identity back together. And I'm not a magician. I've got Humpty Dumpty shattered on the floor of my office, and I can't find the crazy glue and masking tape. So, I gotta get busy looking.

That is why my fear, in the long run, is that if Julian can't be made whole again, he'll leave her.

If she won't let him be whole again, he'll redeem his identity—but not with her. He'll leave and find someone else that'll give him a clean slate. He doesn't realize it yet, but he's on the biggest journey of his life. Only Vanessa holds the map and the keys. What I need to hit Vanessa over the head with—and it's going to feel like I did—is that if she wants to keep the marriage alive, she has to see him as a good man again.

No one who's ever cheated, women included, will stay with someone if they don't feel like they can be seen as a good person again. They will leave because every single one of us has to have the respect and admiration of our partner. And so, while his journey is to win back her respect and admiration, hers is one of forgiveness. Forgiveness on the deepest level. Because how can anyone have respect and admiration for someone who betrayed you and broke your heart like Julian did Vanessa?

When it comes to healing from infidelity, you have to understand what that journey looks like. It's going to look different for the betrayer and the betrayed. Julian's is a journey of self-inflicted choice. Vanessa's is one of forgiveness—and one that's been thrust upon her, I might add. His seems easy and hers far more difficult. But the question of who has it harder pales in importance to the question they now face together.

How do they reclaim the meaning of their marriage?

This is the point in our first session where I wrap up with a short talk on faith: faith in your marriage.

"Right now is a good time to reconnect with the faith you once had in your marriage," I said to them.

"Next session, I'll show you where to go from here. But if you're looking for tools instead of faith, then what I have to say won't matter. You won't have the stamina to apply them."

Vanessa and Julian need faith that their marriage can be beautiful again more than they need a roadmap for forgiveness. A roadmap is simply a set of rules, tools, and obligations. And it requires consistency, something that doesn't come naturally to most people. Me included.

I fall short all the time. Just ask my wife.

The tools you need to save your marriage are just things you do. But the spirit of marriage lives inside of you. In the same place where faith does. That's where you'll find the belief that joy can follow pain.

You don't need tools for that. You need faith.

Right now, the impossible task is getting Vanessa and Julian to believe their marriage can be saved. I'm not saying it's going to be easy. Or even that it should be saved.

Not everyone wants to save a marriage after infidelity. But that's not my call to make.

If Vanessa wants to make it work, that's what I'm here for. Will it be hard? Of course. Does that mean it's bad? Not at all. In fact, their marriage can grow stronger because of betrayal, not in spite of it, assuming Julian never betrays her again.

Right now, Vanessa is feeling like staying is more painful than leaving. Of course it'll feel that way—the pain is triggered every time she thinks of what Julian did in that hotel room that night. But there's immeasurable pain for her if she doesn't grow.

Her plan, like all of our plans, doesn't have to be a plan for more pain. It can be a plan for growth and rediscovery. But it'll still be a plan that requires tremendous courage if she's going to rediscover that joy with Julian again.

Like all of us, Vanessa won't grow if she lacks faith in her marriage. If she doesn't believe that she can forgive, she won't.

There is only one path to forgiveness, and it's riddled with the pain of learning to see Julian in a new light. Not only will she need faith that she can forgive, but she'll need to have faith that Julian can be forgiven. If she lacks the courage to have faith, she'll turn her back on growth. And that won't end well.

So, if she's going to turn her back on anything, it must be on the fear of failure. If she commits to learning, she will learn. If she commits to healing, she will heal. Failure doesn't have to be an option if she doesn't let it be. It'll only be an option if she decides to end the journey.

And with that, I'll leave you with the question I left with Vanessa and Julian:

"Are you willing to learn to forgive and grow—even if you don't know how yet?"

I couldn't get a good read on what Vanessa was feeling about the session when she stood up to leave. She wasn't smiling, and I understood why. I'm not sure I'd be convinced that any amount of therapy could save my marriage after discovering what she did. But she did say thank you. And that she'd come back next week.

I took that as a win and raised my eyebrows at Julian to let him know he should do the same.

Let's Pause Here...

Most couples in crisis think they need more insight into what's wrong with their relationship. They think that if they could just understand why this all happened, everything would start to make sense.

Unfortunately, a decade of experience in this field tells me it won't. In the early stages of a crisis, when the entire meaning of a relationship is being called into question, asking why someone did what they did doesn't make it less painful.

If anything, it makes it worse. Because it keeps you connected to what you don't want: the wound. And so when the wound is open and fresh, don't analyze it. Stop the bleeding first. That starts with a decision. Not with a plan or more tools. And certainly not with knowing "how."

Make a decision to move forward—together—even though you have no idea what that's supposed to look like.

None of us know exactly "how" a marriage is healed. We don't have to. The "how" reveals itself—but only after the fact. That means the first step isn't understanding more. The first step is willingness. Being willing to forgive. To mature. To become someone new in your relationship.

And what fuels that willingness? Faith. Faith that a better relationship is possible. And faith that you can build it. But without faith, nothing I say to any couple will matter. No strategy will stick. No conversations will change minds.

Right now, only two things matter: forgiveness and maturity.

I don't expect you to answer this question right away, but asking this is an important step in that process:

"Are you willing to learn to forgive and grow—even if you don't know how yet?"

Unfortunately for Vanessa and Julian, I can't make them answer yes to that question. That's something they'll have to decide for themselves.

Chapter 2

Feeding the Pain Makes It Grow (Choosing Trust and Forgiveness Before You Know How)

One of the first things people do after cheating on their spouse is quit drinking. Julian was no different. He hadn't touched so much as a beer in the last three weeks. Good for him, I thought. It makes you wonder where we'd be if he'd had that resolve back in Vegas. You have to give him credit, though. He was trying. Hard, too. That's what treading water looks like when you've deeply hurt the one you love.

"Things are better this week," he said after sitting down. "There's still a lot of anger and sadness but less than last week."

The well is probably running a little dry on the tears. The second session always starts off like this. After the initial session, when the tears slow to a trickle and the numbness begins to wear off, hope begins to poke its head through the clouds. I'm about to find out if that's the case here.

"How are you feeling since our last session?" I turned to Vanessa.

"Deep down, I still feel hurt. There's still a wall up, but it's not getting any higher," she offered. "I flip flop between loving him one moment and hating him for wrecking our life the next."

"I understand," I said, but much as I'd love to, I have no idea what she's going through.

It's in these moments I feel like a complete imposter. It's my job to have empathy for others. And I like to tell myself I'm good at it.

But truly understanding her pain? No, I can't. It hasn't happened in my marriage.

"I can't even begin to know the right words to use right now," I admitted. "But, before we dive into all that, do you mind if I ask you something?" I need her buy-in for what comes next.

"Sure, by all means," she responded with reluctance.

"I know your tank's mostly empty," I began. "And what I'm about to ask is going to sound completely insensitive. But, do you think we could hit 'pause' on what hurts for a moment?"

"I want to come back to it a little later, if that's okay," I said, knowing full well I'm going to kick it down the road.

As harsh as that sounds, if we start with what hurts, this session will go sideways real quick.

"What do you mean, pause?" she asked.

"A pause, as in we shoot a tranquillizer into that elephant and spend a moment or two talking about that wall not growing."

I'm not five minutes into our second session together, and I've got a choice: Do I focus on Vanessa's pain or do I ignore it?

Here's the thing: I'm not in the pain management business, and I don't want to be. I'll leave that to the doctors.

The fact that Vanessa's wall isn't getting any higher is huge. It's far more important than you might think. Most people would completely miss this point—therapists included. If her wall isn't getting any higher, it means we've reached the moment when the surgeon walks into the waiting room and says, "Surgery went well. She's stable now."

So, I'm making the conscious decision to steer clear of Vanessa's pain. Not because I'm cold. I know she's been through a lot. You can see it on her face and hear it in her voice.

I'm avoiding the pain right now because doing anything else would be a huge disservice to this couple. Right now, Vanessa and Julian need someone in the room who doesn't just see anger, shame, embarrassment, and grief. They need someone who can see what their relationship could be.

Since that's my job, I'm not focusing on the hole in Vanessa's heart. I'm looking for ways to stitch it back up.

After all, Vanessa is in survival mode. How could she not be?

Will she ever feel safe with Julian again? Will she heal? And what about Julian; will he ever feel like a safe space for her?

If I focus on their pain, I'm inviting more negative emotions into the room. That will dysregulate their nervous systems for the next 50 minutes and turn their pain into something far heavier: grief.

Have you ever helped someone through grief? I have. It doesn't take hours, like I have with these two clients. It doesn't even take days. It usually takes months.

Why is that?

Because grief and talking about grief shuts down a person's ability to access their higher faculties. They become overly emotional. They trade responsiveness for reactivity.

I need to keep Vanessa and Julian's feet firmly planted on terra firma if I have any hope of continuing a conversation in which they'll have unfettered access to their creativity, imagination, will, perseverance, and problem-solving faculties.

"I just don't know if I can do that right now," Vanessa came back at me.

"I completely get that," I replied. "But, right now, whether you realize it or not, I just saw a sliver of hope enter the room."

"How so?" Vanessa asked.

"Let me put it this way. If infidelity can build a wall, something in your relationship is keeping it from getting any higher," I said. "And we could waste our time talking about that wall—how tall it is, how thick, what it's made of. But we'll be living on borrowed time if we do that. We need to focus on getting over it instead."

Julian looked at Vanessa, but her face showed him nothing.

"But you won't do that if you let that elephant stay awake," I said. "You have to put the pain down."

"What you focus on grows," I said. "Every personal growth guru in the world will tell you that."

They looked at each other.

"If we focus on the pain right now, you guys are going to hold onto it like it's your identity. And when you do that, you won't let me tear it out of your hands."

"How so?" Julian asked.

"You only have to hear someone say, 'My marriage is broken' to know they're locked in a fixed mindset," I answered. "Their choice of words will tell you they don't see much good left in it."

"I can see that," he said.

"Right now, we're here because you built a wall between you. It's been under construction for quite some time. We'll get to why later. For now, it's enough to know that you were building it."

I paused to slow things down.

"Today, I'd like to talk about what's on the other side of that wall, if we have any hope of tearing it down. If you don't know what you're fighting for, I promise you, you won't be motivated to fight."

It's at this crucial point in therapy that every couple has to make a decision. Do we stay in this place of pain, or do we move on from here? You'd think that since Vanessa and Julian are in my office, they've decided to move on. But I'm not convinced they understand what 'moving on' truly means.

They say they want their old relationship back. But what they don't realize is that they can't go back. That village is gone—it doesn't exist anymore. Genghis Khan and his hordes burned it down. Their past is now littered with the ashes of the relationship they torched.

Of course, Vanessa didn't torch it. But she did play a role. She may not have lit the damn thing, but she was in the relationship. How do I know? Because Julian said so. He had told me that their sex-life had been hit-and-miss since the girls were born. She could be critical of his parenting yet stingy with her praise when he got things right.

Does any of that justify Julian's decision to step outside of his marriage? Absolutely not.

And at this moment, I'll be the last one to drop his issues with their relationship in her lap. That's going to have to wait for later sessions. But for the sake of this session, we've got a wall to climb, and since I'm about three decades out of SEAL training—or so it feels—I don't need an anchor-like pain swinging from my leg. Nor do Vanessa and Julian.

So, since I can't focus on the pain right now, where can I turn my attention? That's the million-dollar question. And the only correct answer is "forgiveness and trust," the only two topics any good therapist would allow their clients to talk about at this stage of the therapy process.

"I asked you guys last week if you are willing to learn to forgive and grow—even if you don't know how yet. Can I take your pulse on how you feel about that?"

"I'm not there yet," Vanessa replied. "And I don't know if I'll ever get there. Forgiving him sounds nice. Cute, in theory. But, I just don't know. Am I supposed to let it go? Like, sure, that would be great."

I'm not getting a good feeling about this. This is going to be harder than I'd hoped for.

"I'm never going to look back and be like, oh yeah, this is all forgiven. Like, no. Fuck no. Things are not forgiven," she continued. "I don't know if forgiveness is something I'm ever gonna achieve. I'm not a forgiving person."

Did you catch that? Vanessa's forming an identity of herself in her mind and so I've got to walk lightly here. I can't challenge her too much. If I do, I'll just push her to hold onto her position even tighter.

"I get that," I began. "But, if I think of the girls for a second, it's hard to imagine anything they can do that, in your mind, wouldn't be forgivable."

"Yeah, sure, I'd forgive them," she retorted. "Like, if they hurt someone, forgot to call me back, or called each other a name, of course I could forgive them."

"I'm glad you said that. So you're a forgiving person then," I came back with. "Because to say you're not a forgiving person wouldn't be accurate, am I right?"

"I didn't say I was an extremist," Vanessa replied. "But there's things that just aren't forgivable. Like sleeping with hookers while you're on a business trip."

"So now we're talking about a scale," I said. "Like, there are some things that are forgivable and things that are not?"

"Exactly," she said.

"I got it. So what Julian did doesn't fall on the 'forgivable' side of that scale," I continued. "Is that because what he did was so wrong that it can't be forgiven? Or because you don't know how to forgive him for that?" I probed further.

"Both," she replied. "But it doesn't really matter because what he did is not forgivable in my book."

"I'm glad you mentioned the word *book*," I said. "Because if there are things in your book that aren't forgivable—and some things are—then we could, in theory, spend a little time rewriting the book to see if we could alter the scale of forgiveness enough to include what Julian did to you."

"Yeah, maybe," she came back with. "But I don't want to rewrite my book of forgiveness."

"I totally understand that," I replied. "The thing is, if we say this is unforgivable, or irreparable, then we'll stop asking how. We'll stop trying. We'll stop looking for the solution because we don't think we'll be successful in finding it."

"What if I just let it go?" she asked. "So it's no longer in the forefront of my mind."

"That would be one solution," I said. "But would you ever have peace then? I just don't think letting go is gonna be enough for you."

"I've got another solution to present to you," I continued. "What if there was a way to forgive? What if you could find the desire to forgive? What would that mean to you?"

And with those questions, it's a good time to hit pause on the dialogue so I can tell you what's going on here.

Like I said, Vanessa is struggling. She's struggling to envision a future in which Julian can be forgiven and they can have a happy marriage. Her pain is getting in the way, just like I told you.

But the reality for these two is that it's in their pain that they can find growth.

If Vanessa doesn't see herself as someone who can forgive, her path forward narrows. She'll believe her pain will live on for the rest of their relationship. And she won't live like that indefinitely. She'll leave long before she's old and gray.

So, if she believes those statements about herself—that she can't forgive—we're done here. But I'm not going down without a fight. I'll happily square off against Moby Dick. And you can bet I'm going to be obsessed with taking him down.

What Vanessa doesn't realize is that I believe people are inherently good and inclined to grow. I believe Vanessa can grow. And I know for a fact that Julian wants to.

And so I have to believe that Vanessa can learn to forgive. But she'll need to find the desire. She's fragile now, but when I work on Julian next, I have a good feeling that the crack in the door can widen enough to let a little more light in.

"You guys are two people who have a lot of love for each other," I said, looking at Julian, preparing him to tag into our conversation.

"Now, I know there is a lot of pain here," I continued. "But, what if two things could exist for us at the same time? Would it be possible for you, Julian, to start rebuilding trust while Vanessa works on finding forgiveness?"

"Of course. I'd love nothing more than the chance to do that," he replied to my soft pitch.

"You guys have separate missions right now," I continued. "Julian, while Vanessa is deciding whether or not she can forgive you, you want to be asking yourself: how can I rebuild the trust in this marriage?"

"Now is a really good time to remind Vanessa you want to spend the next 40 years showing her…showing your commitment to choosing her."

"That's all I want to do," Julian responded. "I just don't know how."

"I'm really glad you said that, Julian," I said. "You don't have to know how. If you did, we wouldn't be here."

I'm going to hit pause here because I've got a really important point to make.

Julian does not need to worry about how he'll earn Vanessa's trust back—at least not yet. That comes after he commits to the mission of winning it back in the first place.

If you dropped me at the foot of Everest, I couldn't tell you how I'd reach the summit. It'd only be after I stood on its peak that I told you how I did it.

The real work isn't figuring out how to make it up the mountain. It's deciding to make the climb in the first place. Right here in my office, Vanessa and Julian have an identity-level decision to make. Are they the kind of people who are going to fight for their marriage when things get brutal? Or do they walk away?

If Vanessa chooses forgiveness, she'll have to learn how. And if Julian chooses to rebuild trust, he'll have to learn how.

It's the decision to learn that will transform their marriage—and one that marks the real start of the repair.

The *how* is simply a to-do list and one that will reveal itself along the way. Don't get me wrong, the *how* is important; it's just not the first step.

This opens the door to the next important question to ask at this stage of the process: What's in it for them? Why should they embark on their missions of cultivating forgiveness and trust?

I love that question because it speaks to what motivates people.

And what actually motivates people? The carrot and the stick, that's what.

People do what's best for themselves. In Vanessa and Julian's case, there's no shortage of reasons to keep their marriage alive. They stand to lose a lot in a divorce: access to their kids, financial security, and companionship.

When I think of what the stick can do to a person, I know it isn't good. I don't have to look past my twice-divorced parents to know that isn't a door I ever want to walk through.

The carrot is far more motivating.

Imagine where Vanessa and Julian could be in a month with even a little movement away from the pain and toward something better.

In fact, let's go a little further. What could the next 40 years of curiosity, affection, and warmth mean to them? How beautiful could their marriage be if they can forgive, grow together, and show up differently for each other?

It could be beautiful. Even healing.

As I wrapped up our session, the path forward for Vanessa and Julian was clear and hopeful. But pain doesn't like progress. It'd rather derail them than let them believe things can get better.

Pain will also make it hard for Vanessa to push the image of Julian and that woman in his hotel room out of her mind. That's to be expected.

I'm not going to ask Vanessa to forget what happened. But if she wants to forgive him, she needs to put the pain down first. If she doesn't, it'll weigh her down like an anchor—and Julian, too.

What they need is hope. And only forgiveness and trust can provide that.

I instruct them to take out a piece of paper and write on it the word *pain*.

Then they're going to take that word, as it's written in black and white, and put it in their dresser drawer. So they can take a break from what's hurting them and open their minds up to forgiveness and trust.

Once they've done that, I'm going to tell them to look into their empty hands, where they just held pain, and ask:

Vanessa: How can I cultivate more forgiveness for Julian?

Julian: How can I show Vanessa she can trust me?

By asking them to focus on what they want, I'm moving them in the only direction that matters: forward.

As they leave the room, I'm looking forward to next week. I'm excited to help them save their marriage knowing their two beautiful daughters will grow up in an intact family home.

Let's Pause Here...

Because what I'm about to share is advice that's built an entire personal development industry: what you focus on grows.

Pain and joy aren't just emotions you find in marriage. They are identities.

Do you consider your marriage overwhelmingly pain-filled? Or joy-filled?

My marriage? Yes, it's painful at times. I'd still never call it pain-filled.

My wife and I know trying to eradicate pain is a fool's errand. So we don't. We turn the volume down on it.

That's because pain makes you reactive.

I hope that if your marriage is in trouble, you're reading this book with your spouse.

But if not, that's okay. It takes only one of you to anchor yourself to these four things to bring back the creativity, problem-solving, and imagination your marriage needs:

- Hope can be found in situations that aren't getting any worse. If that wall between you isn't getting any higher, then things are stable.
- There's no going back to the old "us," so don't bother trying. What lies ahead is the relationship you deserve—so go after it.
- Focus on what you're fighting for. If you don't know what that is, you can't build it.
- Forgiveness and trust are the only conversations that matter.

And remember from Chapter 1, don't waste your time asking *"How can we repair this?"*

Instead ask:

"Am I willing to forgive?"

"Am I willing to earn back trust?"

Remember, the *how* will reveal itself.

But only if "yes" is your answer—to both.

Chapter 3

The Message You Send (Your Words and Actions Make Them Feel Chosen)

"I shouldn't have trusted him. But who has time to think about your husband cheating on you when you've got two babies hanging on you 24/7?"

That was the first thing that came out of Vanessa's mouth when they sat down in my office. No hello. No small talk. Just the kind of directness that tells me Julian's got some work to do.

"You make a good point," I said, affirming her pain.

Here we are, we just sat down, and I haven't even asked them what's been better this week. I'll give her some room to let off some steam. But not too much. If we stay here long, it's going to be hard to redirect this session toward anything positive.

Most people don't realize—some therapists included—that there's a risk in letting problem-talk dominate the session. It'll make them think that lack of communication is the issue, but it's not. Julian didn't lose his ability to communicate to a bad bet in Vegas. And clearly, Vanessa hasn't lost her voice either. What they need to learn is how to use their words for one thing: to repair what's been broken.

"What made you lead with that?" I began. "We just started, and you're already taking shots at Julian."

"I keep waking up feeling miserable," she replied. "I can't get out of my head what he did. Is he thinking of her? Was she prettier than me? In better shape? I just wish my husband wasn't a cheater."

And there it is, my opening.

Vanessa doesn't realize it yet. But she just showed me exactly where I need to take this.

The second someone tells you what they don't want, they quietly reveal what they've been deeply longing for instead. I'm not going to rush in, though. I let her words hang in the air. This isn't something to manhandle; it's something to white-glove. She's handed Julian the keys to her unlocking her pain, and now it's my job to show him which door they fit.

"That's a really hard place to be," I said, aligning with her. "Anyone would struggle to push that out of their head. The thing is, if we spend all our time today talking about not being able to trust Julian, you're going to leave here thinking the shoe is going to drop again tomorrow. And every time you look at Julian, you'll be thinking, "there's that 'piece of shit' again," if I borrow his words. Do you follow me?"

"I do. But I see the triggers all day, every day. And they hurt."

"I'm glad you said that," I said. "Then you've just confirmed to me that you're looking for the wrong thing."

"Come again?" she said with a confused look.

"I'm going to be blunt here for a second, so don't hate me for it," I began. "You've blown a tire in the middle of the highway, with two infants wailing in the backseat. You're stuck in survival mode, looking in the rear-view mirror, when really what you want is a path forward. And that's what keeps people stuck: obsessing over what they don't want instead of running toward what they do want."

"Excuse me?" she said with a tone that could have grown a hand and slapped me in the face.

"I'll explain," I began. "But, this will require you to let go of the fixed mindset that's keeping you locked in on the pain. Are you ready for that?"

"Yes, of course. I'd love nothing more," she said, softening.

In Vanessa's mind, she's reduced their entire relationship, Julian included, down to a set of binary questions: Can he be trusted—or not? Will he be faithful—or not? Is their relationship salvageable—or not?

In her mind, Julian is either the hero or the villain.

But people aren't static. They're more likely to change than not, often for the better but sometimes for the worse.

Not only can Julian change, he likely will. I know that because I'm living proof. If you'd told my wife that one day I'd learn to be less harsh, she'd have asked what you were smoking.

So sitting here with Vanessa and Julian, I'm asking her to reject that kind of binary "either/or" thinking. It works well for politicians and their lobbyists, but not for married couples. What they need is "and/both" thinking.

Julian can be a loving, kind, generous husband *and* have made a grave mistake. He can spend quality time with Vanessa and the girls; have talked about their goals, careers, and futures together; *and* have stepped outside of his marriage. Let me ask you: What box do you put him in for that? More importantly, what kind of a box does Vanessa put herself in with that thinking? "I can either learn to trust him again or I can't. I can be a forgiving woman or I can't."

Can you see the damage a fixed, black-and-white mindset can have on a person? Or in a relationship? It should be as obvious as the midlife crisis parked in my driveway.

The first step in Vanessa's healing journey is to reject binary thinking. Neither Vanessa nor Julian should want anything to do with it.

And would Julian even find the motivation to do the work required, if he thinks he can never be forgiven? If he sees no other option than to be "the cheater" for the rest of their relationship, he'll stop fighting for it altogether.

So, after putting down the pain and opening the door of forgiveness, the next step in their repair process is to ask:

"Can you entertain the idea that Julian can make a mistake and still be trusted again?"

Or:

"Can this marriage be in crisis and still be repairable?"

Let me drop a few more mind-benders for you to contemplate:

"Can good people do bad things from time to time?"

"Can I be both angry and loving at the same time?"

"Could someone who hurt me so much still love me?"

"Can I still feel joy if I'm in pain?"

For anyone falling asleep in the back of the lecture hall, the answer to all of those questions is a resounding yes.

Indeed, we can all feel two things at once. We can all see hope in a crisis filled with despair. But we won't see hope if we give in to our pain. If we abandon all agency and decide we're powerless in the face of hurt and despair, we lose the ability to ask ourselves the most important question:

"How would I rather feel instead?"

For Vanessa, the moment she discovered Julian's transgression, the pain and hurt from the betrayal slammed the door on the possibility that hope, change and repair is possible. And so now all she sees is a future with

Julian that she doesn't want. A future without options. A future together that cannot be anything other than painful.

That kind of binary thinking will rob her (and Julian) of the hope for change.

Landing this starship back on Earth, I asked Vanessa, "Can you entertain the thought of seeing Julian as someone you can trust just long enough for me to convince him he can earn your trust back?"

"I suppose I can try," she replied.

"That's all I'm asking," I said, relaxing a little into the thought that she's opening the door to forgiveness and letting a little bit more light in.

"I'm not expecting miracles," I continued, pacing her so she doesn't feel pushed too far or too fast. "But I'd love the chance to hear from Julian what he thinks he could do to earn your trust back."

And like the cold-caller that stopped the prospect from hanging the phone up, I turned to him.

"Julian, how did Vanessa win the competition?"

"Come again?" he replied.

"What was it about her that said you wanted to be with her?" I asked, clarifying. "What made her the girl you wanted? I only ask because I'd love to know what made you think she was the one."

"Well, I, uh..." He turned and looked at her.

"I was 30 minutes late for our first date. Back then, we didn't have cell phones. So I couldn't even call her to tell her."

Vanessa cracked a little. Her lips started to curve as she looked at him.

"I was so mad leaving work that I didn't have time to change out of my suit," he continued. "I kept thinking she was going to be turned off. I was over-dressed. Late. Already screwing things up."

He glanced at me and smiled.

"But she wasn't mad at all. When I finally saw her, she was just standing there. She didn't look impatient or annoyed. She looked like a ballerina, hair pulled back, composed, perfect posture."

He turned back to Vanessa. "I remember thinking, *she's the most beautiful woman I've ever seen.* I knew instantly I was meeting my wife for the first time."

The room went quiet.

Before you ask why asking Julian about what made Vanessa a good catch in his eyes has anything to do with winning her trust back, I'm going to give you the rhyme to my reason.

This is going to be some Jedi mind stuff I'm about to share with you guys.

The second I asked Julian what it was about Vanessa that made her the one, she immediately looked at him. We've been at this for three weeks, and Vanessa had yet to give Julian so much as a glance throughout our entire process. The fact that she looked right at him as he began to speak tells me, and should tell you, that there's a message out there that she desperately wants to hear.

The only message Vanessa wants to hear is that Julian chooses her.

In the therapy world, we talk about intervening. That means the questions we ask are thought of as interventions. Tools we use to intervene in the thought processes of our clients. And that's what our clients are coming to us for. They seek our help in breaking the negative thought processes and cycles they find themselves in.

So far, in this session, I've thrown a curveball at Vanessa. Not just once. Twice. I've asked her to reject the pull of the fixed mindset, and now I'm asking her to bear witness to Julian's confession of what makes her a good catch. Can you follow the breadcrumbs?

Vanessa is right here, right now, struggling to believe she's a good catch. And it's Julian, through his transgression, that planted that horrible seed of self-doubt. The second she looked at Julian, the doubt I saw in her almost made me fall out of my chair. If Vanessa were playing poker, she'd be terrible. She gave away her entire hand. And to me, as their therapist, that's pure gold. I couldn't have timed that question any better.

How so? Let me explain.

When someone has been so deeply wounded by their partner's infidelity, they look in the mirror to find the reason why. They blame themselves.

"I'm not attractive enough."

"I wasn't good enough."

"What's wrong with me?"

These questions are what I call filling in the blanks.

When someone wants to know why their partner cheated, they always come back to "because I was/wasn't...."

It's how the mind works: it wants the "why." Why did he cheat? The problem is that nothing the unfaithful partner can say will adequately answer that question. Everything they say will sound like it's coming from Charlie Brown's teacher—wah, wah.

So my task is crystal clear now. Help Julian undo the damage he caused to Vanessa's self-image. He has to cut through the self-doubt she's now saddled with and send the message she's desperate to hear: that she's wanted.

That she is, at her very core, choosable.

"Julian, when things went sideways," I said, deliberately reframing what happened. "Vanessa received a message no woman wants to hear. And if you don't send her the one she does want, the twinkle in her eye is going to disappear. In fact, it's already starting to dim—you've no time to waste."

I think of Russell Crowe playing the whistle-blowing scientist in *The Insider*. If you told me 30 years ago that I'd be quoting that movie in my work, I'd have called you crazy.

But in the movie, he says Big Tobacco isn't in the cigarettes business; they're in the nicotine delivery business.

So why am I telling you about a movie from 1999? Because everything we say and do for our spouse is simply a delivery mechanism for the message we want them to receive. And right now, I need Vanessa—and more importantly Julian—to understand that.

You want your wife to feel special? Instead of making her plan her own date night, hand her a dress and heels and tell her to be ready in 30 minutes.

Want your husband to feel secure? Close your DMs to random men.

Your behavior, which includes everything you say, sends and/or amplifies the message you want your partner to receive. Your behavior is nothing more than a conduit for that message. It's as simple as that.

Fortunately for Julian, Vanessa is still here. She hasn't filed for divorce. That means he's got time. The door is open. Maybe only a crack, but there is light coming in. That can mean only one thing: Vanessa is still interested in receiving messages from Julian. But it's up to him to decide what those exact messages are. Before I dress Julian down one more time for his behavior back in Vegas, I've got two questions I want him to burn into his brain. And he better be asking himself every day for the foreseeable future:

- What message does Vanessa want to receive from me?
- How am I going to send that message?

This is a simple, pragmatic exercise I'm giving him. The same one I'd give anyone who's made a mess of their marriage. I expect nothing less than a smile and follow-through from him. He's also going to repeat these questions out loud, so Vanessa can hear them, right here in the therapy room.

If Julian wants to buy time to repair, Vanessa needs to know that he's embracing this like a spiritual assignment.

Like Noah, he has to start building, no questions asked. That includes having the discipline to keep asking himself these questions. Because the moment he stops, he'll lose the motivation to find the answers—and with it, Vanessa's spark.

Shifting gears, I've got only about five minutes left in our session, and my work with Julian is not quite finished. I still need to help him piece his dignity back together, and the only way I can do that is if he can manage to believe in himself again.

"His dignity? Whaaat?" I can almost hear you say.

Remember, Julian carries a lot of shame for what he did. It's one thing to be cheated on, but that's something that happens to you. Cheating on Vanessa is something Julian did, and that is a reputational transgression he's going to have to live with for the rest of his marriage. So, yes, I need to illuminate a path forward for Julian that will allow him to reclaim a positive self-image. The trouble is, he's going to resist my efforts to convince him that he is very much still a good husband, father, and man.

"Julian, I'm sorry, but I've got more work for you to do this week," I began. "I'm going to need you to use your analyst brain and model out the best version of yourself."

"Model out…the best version of myself?" he hesitated. "Can you explain that a little?"

"Of course. I had a young client once, a computer programmer for a fintech company. He loved the money he was making at his job but hated the actual work. Deep down, he really wanted to make music. Beats, he called it," I shared.

"The thing is, as much as he loved making his beats, he never felt he could give up his day job to turn music into a full-time career. He struggled with self-doubt. Not a twang of it, loads of it. He struggled so much that he viewed his dream of being a musician as completely out of reach."

"But what he didn't understand was that there was no flaw in his passion for music. His talent for it. Or even his love of it. The flaw was his own negative self-image. And because of that flaw, he never attempted to turn his passion into his career."

"Right now," I continued, "If you have any doubt about being the kind of husband you want to be…father you want to be…or the marriage you want to have, I can promise you, you will never become or have what you were meant to."

"There is no flaw in you, your love for Vanessa, or even your love for yourself," I said. "But right now, if you can't tell me what makes you a good husband, father, and man, I can promise you, you'll never become one."

I paused to let him absorb that.

"So use that pen of yours and fill a page with your successes—as a man, husband, and father. Tell me your skills, your talents, and all about the goals you've accomplished. Introduce me to the good man inside of you. Show me what makes him great."

Julian sat 2 inches taller.

"What are you proud of? That's the question that I want answered."

I kept going, even though our time had run out.

"You, Vanessa, and I are building a model. A model of who you are. But we need to feed it good data, or we get bad results. It's garbage in, garbage out," I continued. "That's why I don't need you walking around all day with your head down."

"And Julian, you have to trust me on this: as much as Vanessa would love to see you pay for what you did, there's no benefit to her if her husband is filled with shame. And none for your girls either."

I really needed to wrap up our session, but I had one final thought I needed to share.

Vanessa is never going to put her trust back into a boy.

She's only ever going to give her heart and trust to Julian if he behaves like a man—and a mature one at that. As a boy stuck in a man's body, Julian committed an egregious error in his marriage.

In our next session, it'll be Vanessa's turn to answer for her shortcomings. But for now, they need help exhaling the pain of the adultery; otherwise, there will be no room in their lungs to breathe in what repair and forgiveness can provide.

The only way Julian (and Vanessa) find the source of that oxygen is by rediscovering the good that lives inside of him. That's what this last assignment is all about. It's about moving him from a place of shame, pain, and self-doubt to conviction, self-love, and an unwavering belief in his ability to be the man Vanessa needs him to be.

The question that should live in his mind is:

"When am I behaving like the mature man I know *I can be?"*

Rather than looking back on his faults, which will keep him stuck and drifting sideways, Julian must work toward self-actualization. That's the psychological process of realizing his full potential. Simply put, he must become the best version of himself.

To do that, he can ask himself at the end of the day:

"When did I feel like a good man today? What did I do? And how *did I do it?"*

By connecting with parts of himself that he can be proud of, Julian will find the motivation—and discipline—to make the choices befitting of the husband Vanessa deserves. Yes, he cheated on her. But if he can't let go of that identity, he'll never have the strength to grab hold of the one he wants.

Should he stand in front of Vanessa and own his mistakes? Of course.

Should he hold space for her to talk about her feelings, without defensiveness I might add, and all that she cares to process? Absolutely. Every mature man must do that. But, he has to release himself from his self-imposed punishment. He'll never find the stamina to stay in his marriage if he doesn't.

Julian can't scrub the stain out of his marriage.

But if all he sees is a stain, he'll never ask himself how he needs to show up today—for Vanessa, their girls, or their relationship.

By filling his page with all the things that make him a good man, he'll write his own playbook.

A working model of the man he wants to be.

And a guide for how he becomes that man.

Let's Pause Here...

I don't want to gloss over the importance of receiving the message you crave to hear about yourself: you are chosen.

Infidelity inflicts collateral damage on a person because they start questioning if they're enough.

"Am I not attractive enough?"

"Do they have something I don't have?"

No one wakes up in the morning wanting to ask themselves those questions. But they will, when they discover they're married to an unfaithful spouse.

A discovery like that will push your marriage into the either/or trap. Can our marriage survive—or will it fail? My partner is either trustworthy—or they're not.

And it's this exact binary thinking that has the power to destroy your relationship.

What most couples need is to open their minds by using and/both thinking:

- My partner can be both good, *and* make poor decisions.
- I am desirable *even when* I am not at my best.
- I want to be with my spouse, *and* I don't like all the ways they show up in our marriage.

When you open the "and/both" door, the risk of not sending the message they crave to hear is no longer elevated.

What that looks like:

I choose you *and* I don't like what you did.

See how that works? You can send the message they want to hear, every single day, no matter what they have said or done. That's because the focus of your relationship is on the behavior that sends the message while downplaying the behavior that doesn't.

This shouldn't be hard because we do this in other areas of our lives, with our kids, friends, and co-workers alike. I am now asking you to think this way with regard to your spouse. Others would call this grace. I call it sending the message we all care so much about.

As I leave you here, the question to ask at home if you're reading this book together is: Can we love each other more and catalog our mistakes less?

I'm aware that this is a big ask of someone who's been betrayed. But it's one that must find its way back into your relationship, no matter how long it takes.

And if you're reading this book alone—and you're the one who betrayed your partner—you have to feel good about yourself in your relationship if it's to survive. That means reclaiming your positive self-image.

Here's how I'd start:

"What am I proud of about myself?"

"When did I feel like the good woman/man my partner deserves?"

"What did I do to feel that way? And how did I do it?"

Repairing after betrayal takes time. Those questions, asked regularly, will fill your tank. You'll need that fuel to stay consistent and show up. And it's journaling your successes that make that happen.

If you remember anything from this chapter, it's this: everyone has to feel good about themselves inside of a relationship for it to work.

If they don't, especially the one trying to repair, they'll look for a relationship where they can. And that relationship may not be with you.

Chapter 4

Breaking the Pain Loop (Become a Source of Joy Again)

Ask any couple struggling with infidelity to describe their marriage, and they'll tell you it now comes with a huge asterisk. The lack of trust and forgiveness lies dormant like a cold sore, waiting to erupt when you least expect it. It feels like your world is crashing down when you first find out, but over time, it will come to bother you less and less.

Why is that? Because eventually you will stop caring about what it means. And once the meaning has faded, it will no longer be a problem. When you look in the mirror, you will no longer see an asterisk beside your reflection. You will see your whole beautiful self.

That's what couples struggling with infidelity have a difficult time seeing.

Their guilt, shame, and embarrassment make it nearly impossible to see their relationship beyond the pain of infidelity. So for couples like Vanessa and Julian, the path forward is not the elimination of the memory of the affair. They'll never do that.

The path forward is to care less about what the affair says about their relationship.

And how do they go about doing that? By looking for the small signs that tell a different story.

As we opened our fourth session, a month into our time together, Vanessa said something that gave me an opening—and I wasn't about to waste it.

"Something you said last week really hit home," Vanessa chimed in. "I don't know if I'm ready to forgive yet, but I definitely know I want to move on from here."

"I'm really glad you said that," I began. "A lot of couples get stuck not knowing whether or not they truly want change. If that's where you wanted to stay, we'd be in big trouble. But since you're open to it, I'm going to ask my favorite question: what's been better since the last time we met?"

"Well, I've seen a big change in Julian, that's for sure," Vanessa replied, cracking half a smile.

"I'm glad to hear that," I said. "Can you be a little more specific?"

"Before Julian went on his trip, we were barely functioning. He worked so much that by the time he got home, he was drained. Every night, while I was putting the girls to bed, he'd grab a drink and kick his feet up. I felt like I was going to explode from the lack of help I got at home."

"But in the last couple weeks, since he's taken a step back from alcohol, I've seen a big change," she continued. "He's checking in more. Asking about how I'm doing. Helping with meals."

"Sounds like change. Small, but steady," I said, acknowledging his efforts. "And that's moved the needle some?"

I need to plant the seed here: repair isn't something Julian can do on his own. Vanessa needs to see his change. If a tree falls in a forest and no one hears it, did it really fall?

"It did, in fact," Vanessa replied. "The other evening when he walked in the door and gave me a kiss, I asked myself, how can I contribute more to our relationship?"

"Wait, what?!" I said, feeling really hopeful now. "That's a big shift."

"I know what he did wasn't my fault," she continued. "But I decided to focus on what I'm bringing into our marriage, instead of just the endless task lists."

Boom—that rocked me like one of my daughter's glitter explosions. I definitely wasn't expecting her to say that.

But there is something really important here.

A lot of you may hate me for saying this, but doing chores, prepping meals, and scheduling family activities does not create connection. It never has, and it never will.

They're things connected people do for and with one another. They make a household run smoothly, but they sit at the bottom of the scale of human connection. Far lower than activities that trigger laughter, fun, and security.

Still, when these necessary activities are shared in abundance, you've got a healthy relationship on your hands. But if they're barely happening—or filled with tension and friction—then that should communicate something to you, the same way elevated blood pressure piques your doctor's attention.

That makes for a really good segue to the next important tool I need to teach Vanessa and Julian: scaling.

We know that lack of trust and forgiveness are the last things Vanessa and Julian want. They want more joy, laughter, security, and connection.

But let me ask you—can anyone see, touch, taste, smell, and hear joy? What about security? Better yet, does it announce itself when it enters the room?

No. Because those are feelings.

And you can only see the actions that create them. So, to make the vague concrete, I need to help them measure those feelings—and identify the actions that create them in the first place.

"I've got an important tool to share with you. It is going to help you focus on what's working and how to do more of it," I began. "If you were to rate your relationship today on a scale from 1 to 10, with 10 being the best it's ever been and 1 the other end of the spectrum, where would you put it on that scale?"

"I'd be at a 6," answered Julian.

"I'm a 4," Vanessa said without hesitation.

"Great! That means we're not a 5 and a 3," I said, eternally optimistic.

"Most couples fire me when they get to a solid 8.5 or 9," I continued. "We're about halfway there, so let's keep going. If your relationship felt like a 9, what would be different from today? What would I see? What would the girls see? Paint us a picture."

Details matter here—a lot. If I were a fly on their wall, would there be more hugs? Kisses? Or banter throughout the day? Would I see Julian toss a dress on the bed and tell Vanessa to get ready for dinner out because his mom is coming over to watch the girls? Or would I hear about more intimacy happening in the bedroom?

Let me give you a personal example.

Every morning, as I sit down with my fresh cup of coffee and my tin of Zyns to catch up on my DMs, my wife—who wakes up after me—walks into the living room and, without fail, comes straight over to me and gives me a kiss on the forehead. Sometimes she hasn't even brushed her teeth or wiped the sleep out of her eyes. That happens every single day of my life. And it's the kind of thing that tells you our marriage is operating at a 10.

The relationship scale I'm teaching Vanessa and Julian is a compass for their marriage. It helps them track their progress and identify the actions that'll move them further up.

"We're going to take it one step at a time," I said. "So tell me, what would a 7 and a 5 look like for you guys?" I ask.

"Well, I'd be a priority," Vanessa began, not knowing I'm going to press her to give me more than just words.

"Great. But what does that look like?"

"He'd put our relationship above everything. His work. Heck, even our kids," she replied.

"I love that," I started, "but what does that look like? Help me build a real image of that in my mind."

"Well, the other morning after a night of very little sleep, he rescheduled a meeting and stayed home so I could have a sleep-in," she shared.

Bingo. That's what I'm talking about. I'm not letting this nugget slip out of my hands.

"Wait, you're telling me Julian moved his morning around and stayed home with the girls to make sure you could get a little extra sleep?" I asked.

"Yes," she said, shooting him a look and smiling.

"Do you mind if I ask what that says about him? You know, that he wanted you to get that extra sleep?"

"That he loves me. That he cares," she replied.

"Follow my breadcrumbs a little more, will ya?" I began. "If he's the type of man who loves you enough to want to make sure you get a little more rest after a particularly difficult night with the girls, what does that mean to you?"

"It means I'm a priority to him," she said, staying with me.

"And if you're a priority to him, what must that say about you?" I asked, hoping she takes the bait.

"That he wants a life with me. That he loves me. That he wants to be with me," she replied.

"And if you're the woman he wants to be with, what kind of woman must you be to him then?" I said, bringing it home.

"That I'm a woman worth choosing," she said, ignoring the tear that's fallen in her lap.

"Ahh, so that can mean only one thing," I continued. "That you're chooseable."

Right about now is a good time to point out that if Vanessa wants to feel chosen—as she should be—it's going to be contingent upon how cherished Julian feels.

Wherever the origins stem from, nature or nurture, I've come to the conclusion that women want to feel chosen and men want to feel cherished. My opinion here is built on a belief that the lion's share of work done by men in the pre-coupling phase of a relationship is in the pursuit itself. Women, in contrast, work hard post-coupling to affirm the man's decision as correct once she accepts his offer.

I want you to see it as the yin and yang of relationships. Men want to feel cherished, and women chosen. That's not to say that we each don't want the other. Of course, men want to feel chosen and women cherished. But these goals, as I see them, are secondary to the primary goal important to each sex.

Back to Vanessa and Julian and the covenant of reciprocity. When they married, they promised to choose and cherish one another. I need to understand, as does Julian, how cherished he's felt inside of their relationship. I must inform you that in no way, shape, or form am I saying that Julian not feeling cherished by Vanessa in the weeks, months, and years leading up to his transgression in that Vegas hotel room justifies his decision in any way. But Vanessa's answer to this next question is going to provide a ton of context to how fulfilled Julian has felt in their relationship.

"I'm really glad we've identified what's been missing here for you, Vanessa," I started. "Can I ask you, because I'd love to know, have you cherished Julian as much as he deserves?"

"I guess I haven't lately," she said sheepishly.

"Would you say that's done anything to your connection, as a couple?" I asked. "I want you to know that I'm not excusing what he did just because your relationship hasn't been a 10 out of 10 recently. But I do know that if we can understand where the blind spots are, we can check our mirrors and make sure future collisions can be avoided."

"There's been a lot of focus on the kids," she started. "Life's really busy with twins. I suppose I've held back a lot. I do love him and want him to feel wanted, but I haven't had much desire these days."

"What's that done to things like affection?" I asked, being careful with my choice of words. I'm not about to hit a mother of infant twins with a lack of effort in the sex department.

"It's been less. A lot less," she confessed while looking at her feet.

This is the moment. My chance to show Julian how to resuscitate his marriage.

"Julian!" I said, almost shouting. "I need you to take the mic for a second. We're all adults here. Parents, too. You're not going to mistake me for Dr. Phil when I say that the birth of twins is going to throw a monkey wrench in the physical and emotional connection between a couple."

Julian begins to nod.

"The thing is, there are tons of couples in the same season of life who find ways to stay connected," I said.

"Intimacy has faded here," I continued. "What got in the way? Did that happen on purpose? Or was that unintentional?"

"I guess it was a little bit of both, if I'm honest," Julian replied, also staring at his feet. "I didn't really slow down with work as much as I should have, once the girls came," he continued.

"No, you didn't," Vanessa chimed in. "In fact, you did the opposite. You kept going—full tilt—and even pushed back when I asked if my mom could stay past the first month."

"I told you that I was happy she could stay with us," he retorted. "But I wanted to feel important, too. I wanted to be involved. And even after she left, I still didn't feel that way. I went from the third wheel to the fourth wheel—behind you and the girls."

Julian turned to Vanessa and said, "How do you think it feels—being met with nothing but criticism? Do you think it's motivating to be reminded all the time to check if the milk is too hot? Or to be yelled at because you take your eyes off the girls for a second to run into the house and grab something? They were strapped in their car seat. They weren't going anywhere!"

This is going sideways real quick, which is not my intention.

But this is good. This stuff needs to come out. Julian needs a witness right now. He's tired of Vanessa's constant worst-case-scenario future-tripping. It makes him feel like an incompetent dad.

A bad dad. That's it. That's the message that he's receiving.

Remember, we're talking here about a man who's extremely successful. At work. With friends. In life. But to hear that he's failing at fatherhood is going to mess with his brain. It's going to feed his sense of disconnection. That is going to push him to be more successful in the areas where he can find the message that he's a success—namely, at work.

Julian's disconnection is what fuels Vanessa's resentment. He pulls back. She becomes increasingly resentful. As I mentioned, you don't need to be a bald TV talk-show host to tell you that.

"I'm going to stop you guys right here for a moment," I said, interrupting them. "I hear you both. I feel for you. And I'm going to re-orient you."

"Julian, the fact is, you've got dozens of examples of when Vanessa was critical. And critical to the point you pulled away. In anger, frustration, or resentment."

"And Vanessa, you're not lacking in the resentment department either. I'd hold a grudge, too, were I in your shoes. It's not easy with one, let alone two, newborns."

"All that said, you guys are staring down the barrels of each other's pain, and no one has the wherewithal to put down their arms and simply say, I'm sorry." I said in my most firm yet kind tone.

"There's been neglect on both your parts. Work has come first. Kids have come first. Everything has come first, except your relationship."

"And that's the first sin of marriage: not putting it first. The second sin: doing everything else before putting work into your marriage. Did you stop going to bed at the same time? Did impatience get met with a sharp tone of voice? Did someone lose confidence in asking for sex?" I said, probing for affirmation.

By now, their nodding heads clearly communicate that I've got their undivided attention.

"Now, this all happens slowly, over time, in a way you don't even realize it's happening," I continued. "But what you guys have done is gotten yourself tangled up in a pain loop."

"You've become each other's source of pain."

"And simply by virtue of becoming that source of pain, your actions and behaviors toward one another only serve to reinforce that. So, if you want to break out of that pain loop, here's what you're going to say, word for word. And in good faith. Don't even think about pulling a fast one on me. You have to be genuine when you use this script."

And with that, here's word-for-word what I asked Vanessa and Julian to say to each other:

"I hurt you. I don't know how to repair this yet. But that doesn't matter right now. Because all that matters is I want to be a source of joy to you again."

The problem most couples in crisis face is that they can't imagine becoming a source of joy, strength, and healing for one another again.

When that happens, they stop believing their efforts will make a difference—they lose the motivation to try—and they stop asking:

"How can we serve each other, our children, and our family?"

"Before we wrap for today, I need to ask you," I said, winding down our session. "What do you think could happen here, if you sprinkled a little more joy into this relationship?"

I looked at Julian.

"Julian, if you're having trouble here, remember that frown Vanessa has been wearing on her face for most of our sessions?"

"Yeah, I do," he replied.

"Well, what if, when you saw that frown, you remembered that your next move is the Uno reverse? What would change here if you made it your mission to make Vanessa smile today?"

"And Vanessa, what if you were to remind Julian how much he means to you? And tell him what a great job he's doing?"

Vanessa and Julian didn't answer.

"Would Vanessa still have that frown on her face?" I asked Julian.

"Would Julian walk around thinking he's a bad dad?" I said, looking at Vanessa.

"If this was your mission, saying things like 'You look handsome today,' or 'I love you so much' a little more often, would things feel better?"

I let that simmer.

"You know, we tell our kids we love them—at least 15 times a day if you're mine. And that's just before lunch," I said with a laugh. "Don't you think the warm and fuzzies of the honeymoon phase could come back?"

"I can't disagree with you on that," Julian finally spoke up.

"If you're anything like me," I continued, "you know that frowns, hunched shoulders, or clenched fists aren't the goal. It's the light they bring into the room we're after—and the reason no one has to sit alone in the dark."

"So, can you do that for one another? Can you bring the light back into your relationship and be each other's source of joy again?"

And with that, we wrapped up our session. I hope I sold them on accepting that zany mission.

I call it a zany mission only because we tend to treat making our partner feel chosen and cherished like it's a one-time assignment: something done at the altar and forgotten once the honeymoon wears off.

Ideally, I've convinced them that a successful outcome need not be any more complicated than sending each other the message we all want to receive: that we're loved. Cherished. And indeed chosen. In a week, I'll find out exactly how successful I've been.

Let's Pause Here...

There are two ways to feel better about your relationship. One way is to eliminate all the pain (impossible by the way). The other way is to fill your relationship with so much joy you don't care about the pain that never quite seems to disappear completely. No one cares about losing a few nickels when they've got a wad of twenties in their pocket.

"Honey, I don't know where we go from here. But I know we'll get there when we see each other *as a source of joy. And I want to be that source for you."*

That's your simple, actionable script for this chapter. One decision, communicated in a single sentence.

If I wanted you to memorize every word in this book, I'd have trimmed it by 90%. I don't want you to do that. I want to change your mind. I want you to see your marriage as two people standing arm in arm, united against the world, problems included.

When you refuse to be each other's source of pain, you can start moving up the scale toward joy.

Every time you ask yourselves, "What would be happening in our relationship if we were a 9?" you'll seek out ways to send each other the same identity-level message neither of you ever gets tired of hearing: "I choose you."

Chapter 5

Do More of What Works (Pain Hates Consistency, Healing Loves It)

"We made love last night," Vanessa announced at the start of our next session, shooting Julian a smile.

"Wait, what?" I replied, intending to sound surprised. "How did that happen?"

"It was quite unexpected really," she began. "Julian wrapped up a late afternoon meeting and came straight home. On his way, he called to say he was grabbing some takeout for dinner. After dinner, we took the girls for a walk and gave them a bath. He usually misses bath time, so it was nice that he was there."

"I was quite surprised that Vanessa got them to sleep in less than an hour," Julian chimed in.

"Me, too," Vanessa agreed. "I usually have to rotate them back and forth a few times nursing, but I think the walk and long bath time with Daddy tired them out more than usual."

"And so one thing led to the other, and it just happened," Vanessa wrapped up.

"Don't forget the massage!" Julian blurted out. "I like to think I had something to do with it."

"Ahh, you make a good point, Julian," I said, clocking something familiar.

When things are going well in a relationship, people suddenly want their fingerprints all over the outcome. When things aren't going so smoothly, though, they're nowhere to be found. It fills the room the moment someone says, "Don't forget the massage!"

What matters isn't who deserves credit for their effort; it's that a shift has happened. The lesson here—one most couples miss—is what I call *filling the credit gap.*

Shifts like this don't happen by accident.

First, Julian came home from work early. Why would he do that? Was it luck? Happenstance? Or did he consciously decide to show Vanessa where his priorities lie?

Second, his thoughtfulness extended beyond simply walking in the door only to ask, "What's for dinner?" He stopped at their favorite Chinese restaurant. He called ahead to tell Vanessa not to bother cooking. Who does that? A man that's thinking about his wife is who does that.

It's been weeks since Vanessa and Julian were intimate, well before the affair happened. In earlier sessions, Vanessa admitted that she'd pushed Julian away. She was "touched out." Add Julian's transgression to the equation, and it's easy to understand Vanessa's disinterest in intimacy.

And yet, last night, they made love and fell asleep holding each other.

This is a major shift.

Now, my job is to find out exactly what has changed. Because if I don't help them name it, time-stamp it, and drive it deep into their core memories, this moment will quietly slip away...unclaimed and, worse, underappreciated.

Most couples are experts at cataloging pain. Ask 100 couples to describe their relationship, and 99 of them would write me a novel about what's gone wrong. Very few could tell me when things went right—or why.

I need Vanessa and Julian to hear and feel the shift they just made happen. I need them to recognize that they are the ones who initiated it. Not me. Not anyone else. Just them. That is what matters here.

Progress that is noticed can be replicated. That's how you fill the credit gap.

And seeing progress is what will give them the hope they need to believe they can successfully save their marriage.

"Vanessa, I know you've kept Julian at arm's length for quite some time," I began. "But what was it that made you want to be physically close again?"

"It was kind of a snowball effect really," she began.

"When he called on his drive home, there was an excitement in his voice. He said he couldn't wait to spend the evening with us and suggested he grab takeout so we could take the girls out for a walk after we ate."

"After the walk, Julian scooped the girls out of the stroller, carried them upstairs, and jumped in the bath with them," she continued.

"Sounds like fun!" I said.

"They always have fun in the bath," Vanessa said. "I was tidying the living room when I started hearing their laughter. They're so cute when they laugh. You can't help stopping whatever you're doing to see what's so funny."

"I ran upstairs and peeked my head in the bathroom. They were splashing, shrieking, and having so much fun. Julian was right there with them, helping them soak the floor."

Vanessa turned and looked at him. "That's when he looked up at me, smiled, and said, 'I love you.'"

Julian took her hand.

"At that moment, I didn't feel the pain. I felt his love. I didn't see the man who cheated on me. I saw a dad."

"Wow! Something is different!" I replied. "That's a huge shift."

At this moment in the session, I couldn't help thinking of a couple I worked with back when I was an intern.

They came to me about six months into their marriage. The wife said her husband had a drinking problem, and she was fed up with it. Every time he got paid, he gave her half the cost of their rent, food, and utilities. He'd spend what he had left buying as much vodka as he could and drinking it all weekend till it was gone. He'd repeat that every two weeks.

Well, during our second session, I asked him how much he drank in the last week. He told me he didn't quite have enough for his usual two 26-ounce bottles. "That's interesting," I said. "Why didn't you have enough for two?"

He said that Friday, after he got paid, he took their three kids (not his) to eat at McDonald's and then out to the movies. So, he only had enough for one bottle. I thought that was interesting. I wrote it in my notes and made a point to compliment him later in the session for his effort.

Two weeks later, they came back after a family trip to Disney. His wife turned to me and said, "This'll be our last session. Thanks so much for all your help."

"That's amazing. I'm so glad to hear that," I said, happy to be getting laid off from my job as their therapist. "So, what happened while you guys were away? I mean, what shifted?"

"Well, we were in the hotel room, waiting for our shuttle to the amusement park, and I looked over at him playing with our daughter and realized,

I didn't see an alcoholic. I saw a father. A man who was a father to kids who weren't even his own."

I cried when she told me that—on the inside, of course. Just like I cried when Vanessa said she saw a dad, not a cheater.

You see, every single one of us has a choice. And as much as I tell people they get to choose what they see, they need to make that choice on their own. And here was Vanessa making a choice to see more than a cheater when she looked at Julian. Vanessa was choosing to see what she wanted to, not what she didn't.

Will her memory of discovering Julian's prescription and all the events and the details of his infidelity disappear just because she chooses to see a different version of him? Of course not. But can that memory fade? Become less painful? Be eclipsed by the man that sits beside her today? Absolutely. Can the affair be a catalyst for something better? A better marriage? A deeper love? One hundred percent. There's no doubt about it.

"You know, since we're talking about a shift in perspective," I said, not letting go of this huge step forward Vanessa and Julian have taken. "What was it about Julian that made you say yes? I mean, of all the guys out there, what did he have that was so special?"

"I've always loved the way his brain works," she answered with a look of admiration. "I love his wisdom. He just sees the world and people differently. He could always get you to open your mind and think about things from a new perspective."

"Sounds like he's fighting really hard right now to do just that," I responded.

"I am," chimed in Julian. "She means everything to me. They all do."

"I'm so sorry for what I did to you," he said to Vanessa, tears trickling down his face. "I can't erase what I've done. But will you give me the chance to try?"

"I know you weren't trying to hurt me," Vanessa said, throwing Julian a lifeline. "I know you didn't wake up that day thinking 'how can I hurt Vanessa today?'"

"I don't know if I'll ever understand why I did it," Julian interrupted. "But I want to be the kind of man I'd want our daughters to marry. I'm so sorry I wasn't that to you."

"I don't love what you did to me. And I don't want to live with the pain," Vanessa said. "But if living without the pain means living without you, I don't want that either."

"It kills me every time I think about it," Julian turned to me. "It just eats me up inside."

"What if there was one more shift we could make?" I asked.

"What's that?" asked Vanessa.

"What if something like this could be moved into the forgivable category?" I replied. "Not the forgettable category. But the forgivable one?"

"That would mean choosing to frame forgiveness as a choice. A choice you're making for you. For Julian. For the girls. And your marriage."

"To do that, you have to see Julian in a new-old light. The same man you fell in love with and married, but stronger. More weathered. Battle-tested. Better, because of what you've survived."

"How so?" she asked.

"He's still the husband, father, and man he always was," I continued. "Only now he's fighting his own shame, guilt, and self-hate. He's going to have to live with what he's done."

Vanessa shot a glance at Julian.

"But regardless of what he's done, you still get to choose what you see when you look at him. You get to pick the label you want to give him."

"I'm not saying you have to choose this label today, but it'd be a good idea to choose to see him as a good man again, at some point in the future."

"Does that sound like a choice you think you can make?"

You could feel the sigh Julian let out when Vanessa replied, "I think I can. I mean, I want to."

I always say that for therapy to work, you need two willing customers. Do you want a positive outcome? Then both people have to line up to buy what I'm selling. Otherwise, repair is never going to happen. This process doesn't work if you've got one person leaning in while the other is leaning out.

Now, if your partner shows no interest in bettering your relationship, and you're reading this alone, don't panic.

First, don't assume they don't care. More often than not, they lack hope, or they fear blame—or both.

The good news: change is possible, even if they don't participate.

Because no relationship can stay the same when one person changes inside of it.

So instead of focusing on their absence, focus on going first. The best way to engage a "resistant" partner is to show them that you're willing to work within their level of comfort.

If, after all your effort, they still don't show up, then you'll have a different decision to make. But don't get ahead of yourself. There's still a lot you can do before you get there.

And that's exactly what's happening with Vanessa and Julian.

It's taken us five weeks to determine whether Vanessa is signing up for repair or not. If you thought Julian was all-in for repairing their marriage from the start, you'd be correct. But you'd be missing two big parts of the equation. One is his willingness to show up for Vanessa in their marriage in the way she needs him to. And the other is to abandon the debauched version of himself that could ever allow such a thing to happen. Julian always needed to buy into a better version of himself.

Julian will never talk his way into convincing Vanessa to trust or feel secure with him. He'll only do that when his daily mantra is to ask himself, 'How can I show up for her today?'

On top of that, if Julian buys into the belief that he can fulfill his mission of making his marriage work, then he'll find the courage to face his demons and conquer his self-soothing behaviors that damaged his marriage in the first place. He'll reject the late nights. The drinks after work. The prolonged absence from home.

But that requires one thing a man with a mission must embrace: discipline.

Discipline to believe in himself.

Vanessa will need a heavy dose of discipline, too. She'll have to resist the urge to endlessly autopsy Julian's betrayal if she wants to trust him again. Clinging to the old injury will keep them stuck. Choosing to forgive Julian, and seeing him as the man he can be, is not optional. It's the price of admission.

Now, I don't graduate couples because all their problems are solved. I graduate them because they've learned how to choose each other without needing me in the room.

That's why I am going to leave them with another exercise they can do at home. The last one before I turn them loose.

"I'd like to leave you guys with something to think about," I began.

"Yeah, of course," Julian replied, like the nerdy kid sitting in the front row.

"I see couples all day, every day. And one thing that always rubs me the wrong way is how often they'll tell me, 'We haven't been putting in as much effort as we should.' It's like they wear that statement with a false sense of pride. Call me old-fashioned, but I like to live by the words, 'an ounce of prevention is worth a pound of cure.'"

"So going forward," I said, getting to the point, "I want you guys asking yourselves these three questions:

When do I feel forgiveness?

When do I feel trust?

What am I doing to create those feelings?"

"If you want to keep building a life together—one that survives the test of time—you have to stay aware of what you're doing today that's making that happen. What are you doing today that's creating this shift?"

"It's not having all the tools to build that perfect life together that matters. It's the desire to have that amazing life that does."

"Remember this: desire comes first. The how-to follows."

"Anyone can learn to be self-reflective. Forgiving. Disciplined. Honest and transparent. But only if they want to!"

"So keep challenging yourselves to reject a fixed identity that your marriage is broken. That your partner's broken. Or that you're broken."

"Reject that nonsense and keep asking yourselves, 'What version of us will we be in three months, six months, a year, or 10 years?'"

"Always remember that how you repair this is never going to be the largest problem you face. This was never about a how-to problem. It's always been a desire problem."

"And so, if you want that connected, intimate, and forgiving marriage, you have to believe you can build it. Build the image in your mind of what it looks like, and have faith that the how will reveal itself. It always does."

Vanessa turned to Julian, took his hand, and said, "I know you're sorry for what you did. Guilt won't fix our marriage. But we can. I'm ready now."

You could set your watch to the moment a couple decides they no longer need my services. I've seen it hundreds of times.

A couple doesn't need my help getting across the finish line. They need help starting their engine and pushing the accelerator to the floor when the race starts.

Everything I've done during these five sessions with Vanessa and Julian was the warm-up lap. Their race began when they decided to choose to fight for each other. That's what Vanessa was saying to Julian by taking his hand as they left my office.

Julian had been waiting at the starting line for Vanessa, for the chance to prove he could be the man she deserved. The man he knew he could be.

Julian squeezed her hand back. Not with the grip of a desperate man but with a confidence that, together, they would win this race and do a victory lap together.

I don't need them to leave my office and drive off into the sunset toward perfection. There'll still be many hard moments, long talks, and old triggers to face.

But perfection isn't the absence of pain and disappointment. It's the daily decision to choose and cherish the person beside you in the race of life.

As they left my office for the last time, I didn't see a couple stuck in the pits; I saw a couple committed to winning the only race that mattered.

Let's Pause One Last Time...

...before we meet Jada and Chris.

Infidelity will rock any marriage like a stick of dynamite. If I'm honest with you, I'm not sure my own marriage would survive it. I won't pretend to know if Vanessa and Julian's will either.

You can't erase the memory of infidelity. But you can outgrow it if you choose to.

First, by doing more of what works. Nothing builds trust like choosing your partner every single day. And if you're the one doing the forgiving, show them you notice their effort. You are the only one who can tell them it's not in vain.

Second, by resisting the temptation to catalog the pain. That only connects you to what you don't want: more pain.

Third, by remembering that desire precedes progress. Deciding to repair is more important than knowing how.

Fourth, by choosing what you see. The second Vanessa saw a dad, not a cheater, her heart opened.

Fifth, by taking action. If action got you into this mess, action will get you out. Ask yourself: "What am I prepared to do to save this?"

I'd never let anyone leave my office without reminding them that they have the power to create the shifts they want in life.

Remember what I said earlier in the chapter: progress that's noticed is progress that can be replicated.

How you do that is by asking each other:

"When did you feel forgiveness?"

"When did you feel trust?"

"What did I do to create those feelings?"

You'd never get on a plane without knowing the destination. But you couldn't have bought the ticket without doing what it took to pay for it. Most people can tell you how they made that happen. But can they tell you what they did to earn trust and forgiveness after betrayal?

If not, those questions should be the first ones you ask your partner tonight.

I have to believe that the seemingly impossible is possible.

If it wasn't, Vanessa would never forgive Julian, he would never earn her trust, and you wouldn't be reading this book right now.

Because I'd never have written it.

Part II

Jada and Chris: Overcoming Conflict

Chapter 6

What Are You Afraid of? (Trade Fear for the Connection You Crave)

When Jada's ex walked out on their marriage, she became a single mother overnight. Her ex's decision to leave her and her two boys to go and build a life with another woman didn't just hurt. It reopened an old wound: the same one her father left when he walked out on her mother.

Jada had spent her entire life, and vast sums of money in therapy, trying to unlearn the narrative that the men she loves leave because she is unlovable. And now, in her new relationship with Chris, that belief was back, stronger than ever, and threatening to take her through the emotional roller coaster once more.

Jada took her seat after Chris, crossed her legs, and looked me straight in the eye.

"We couldn't be in a worse place right now," she said.

You could see the cortisol dripping from her face. Her wrinkles looked deeper than any makeup could hide. And her shoulders. They never lie. Hers were hunched forward, rounding her back. She was cocooning like she was bracing for another salvo of missiles to land.

The look on Chris' face corroborated her story.

From my early days as an intern, I've loved the challenge of refereeing a couple in crisis. I seem to come alive when the tension in the room rivals that of the border between India and Pakistan.

"So, how did we get here?" I asked.

"I was looking up a recipe on his phone last week," she started. "And that's when I found the deleted messages."

Deleted messages? I thought to myself. I must be a dinosaur because I had no idea you could find deleted messages. Why are they called deleted if you can?

"It was *just* a co-worker," Chris explained. "It didn't mean anything."

Except to Jada it did.

"I was just being friendly," Chris offered. "What was I supposed to do? Ignore her texts? We're just friends! Chill out!"

"Chill out? Why the fuck do I have to chill out at 8 p.m. on a Sunday night?" Jada replied, ratcheting up the tension. "Why the fuck does this bitch think it's okay to message you outside office hours? And why are you deleting anything if you've got nothing to hide?"

Buckle up everyone; here we go. This one's about to get spicy. I'm glad I didn't pop that 6 mg Zyns just before we started. I didn't need the nicotine-induced rush of blood to my head to stay alert for this one. In just that two-minute exchange, I'd gotten all the context I needed; but, to keep it interesting for you, here's more of their back story.

Chris accepted a transfer and moved halfway across the country three months ahead of Jada. They'd met a year and a half prior and had been living together for three months when he took the job. He earned well in tech sales, and the appeal of lower taxes made accepting the transfer a no-brainer. On top of that, their blended family of six needed more room, so a bigger home for less money was another draw. Now all they had to do was last long enough to make it all worth it.

Chris shared custody of his kids with his ex. Since his eldest was a freshman in college and his youngest was starting next year, his role as an active parent was slowing down. And after a costly divorce, the thought of more distance between him and his ex put a smile on his face.

Jada stayed behind with her two boys so they could finish out the term before switching schools. She was a flight attendant, so being based out of a new city wouldn't be an issue for her.

The three months apart felt good. For both of them.

They had amazing chemistry, but things had been rocky from the start. Quietly, they both appreciated the break from fighting and the opportunity it gave them to catch their breath. Despite an intense physical connection and love for one another, they were easily caught in "little traps" that caused them to fight for hours, they said. It sounded to me like quicksand would be a more accurate description judging by how our first session together was getting started.

They both loved being parents and were aligned on how they wanted to raise their kids. So it wasn't their differing parenting styles that had lit the powder keg in their relationship; it was their pasts.

Jada's father leaving when she was young, followed by her ex when her boys were six and three, left her questioning just how "stayable" she was in the eyes of men.

Chris, on the other hand, grew up in a home where the men were made to walk on eggshells by the woman of the house, his mother. The constant state of hypervigilance he existed in left little room for him to feel safe being his true self.

They came into the relationship primed to clash.

Jada led with demands for reassurances that Chris never felt confident supplying. The result? She'd push and he'd stumble—until they both felt like they were dancing on a pinhead, keenly aware that one wrong step would end the performance.

Coming back to the fight that had caused them to contact me, Jada explained that she'd thrown a plate out of anger that night. It shattered on the refrigerator beside him, and a piece of it hit Chris in the head.

The sight of blood woke her up. She ran to the bathroom, found the Steri-Strips, and closed the wound well enough to keep Chris out of the emergency room.

She didn't mean to hurt Chris, but she did.

Jada apologized immediately. She knew the pain she'd carried for years from the men who'd left her was behind her actions, and she promised Chris she'd address it.

It was their first bad fight since reuniting. And while it started off in much the same way as their others, this one ended with someone getting hurt.

Thankfully, their kids hadn't seen anything—they weren't home at the time of the fight.

Once the bleeding stopped and things had settled, Chris turned to her and said, "We're getting help, or I'm done." That's when they called me.

Here's a question I get a lot: Can you do couples therapy when violence has taken place?

The answer is: it depends—on safety and the nature of the violence.

Back when I was an intern, my supervisor explained that there are two main types: the pitbull kind and the cobra kind.

When conflict escalates to the point that someone loses self-control and crosses a line, it's situational—the pitbull kind, as my supervisor called it. It's never acceptable or excusable. It is sometimes possible to work with a couple like this. But only if neither partner is afraid of the other and there's a commitment to never letting it happen again.

In Jada and Chris' case, that's what made it possible for us to proceed. And while I didn't need to consult my supervisor Susan on how to handle this, I did anyway, to protect myself ethically.

A cobra strike, on the other hand, is different. It's calculated, intimidating, and meant to control. When it's present, couples therapy is generally inappropriate. It's not a communication problem—it's a safety issue that requires immediate support.

Were that the case for Jada and Chris, we would not be moving forward with couples therapy.

So what does that mean if you're facing something similar?

If any form of violence has happened in your relationship, get help. A trained professional will work with you to identify your situation and guide you toward the right support.

My work with Chris and Jada was clear now.

Not only do they need real strategies for navigating their volatility, but they've got to commit to a pact of nonviolence and follow a clear safety plan. On top of that, I need them to understand that children cannot witness violence of any kind. If the children see something like this and I become aware of it, I have a legal obligation to report it to child and family services.

To make things more complicated, Chris was threatening to leave if things didn't change.

Chris wasn't expecting it, but I was about to shift the focus of our session away from Jada. I was satisfied she understood the gravity of the situation and was committed to the pact of nonviolence. It was time to focus on what Chris brought to the table.

I can already hear many of you—especially the men—asking, "What the heck? Why are you focusing on Chris when Jada is the one throwing plates in the kitchen?"

Fair question. Let me explain.

I need both of them to calm things down. If anything is going to change, both of them are going to have to get really comfortable with forgiveness and repair.

But none of that will happen if I don't help them build safety on top of a foundation of concrete and rebar. If we try to construct anything on top of sand, it's all going to collapse six months down the road. Maybe a year, at most.

As it sits right now, Jada's stuck in fight or flight. If I don't help her break that pattern, she'll leave here with a teaspoon of insight and a gallon of false hope. That's not my MO; I'm here for real change.

I had to tackle Jada's self-doubt—her belief that she's leavable—or they'd become another case of the 60-plus percent of second marriages that end in divorce.

As much as it was killing me inside to not ask Chris what he was thinking by deleting messages from a female colleague, I held off. I'd hit him with that one later.

"Chris, what tells Jada that she's stayable?"

"What do you mean?" he asked with a confused look.

"As in, how does she know that she's someone you'd want to stay with?"

"I don't know. I never asked myself that question."

"Wouldn't that have been a good one to ask yourself before you hid messages from another woman from her?"

"Now that you put it that way," he began slowly, "I guess I didn't really think much about how it would have come across."

Here's a little more context.

Jada is a flight attendant. She flies short haul. She chose a career that requires her to meet a ton of people every day but never long enough to get to know them.

Then we have Chris. Working in tech sales means that when he's not out of town on business, he's entertaining—a lot. Dinners, golf, conferences, and more golf. It's one of the perks of his job. And it suits him well. He's the outgoing, friendly type. Everyone loves him.

But that's exactly what derails Jada. Although she didn't say this in our first session together, I suspected that it threatened her to no end. He's always on his phone. And likes to refer to his executive assistant as his "work wife." It doesn't take a PhD in human psychology to know that he likes to make people happy because deep down he's scared of making people upset, a wound his mother opened up in him.

When you work in this field long enough, you develop a keen sense of spotting which childhood wounds people walk around with. Jada didn't have to say a word for me to see it. She suffered from the same issue I do: insecurity.

You could see it immediately in the flash of contempt that crossed her face when Chris talked about how much he enjoyed networking and meeting new people. It was so clear that you could read the story her nervous system was writing. Although she was attracted to Chris' charisma, it threatened her. Charismatic men—like her father—are hard to tie down and will eventually leave, she told herself.

There's a hard truth about human behavior: hurt people will do whatever it takes to protect themselves. Raise the stakes emotionally, and they'll sacrifice connection to avoid being confronted by their worst fears. Jada was no exception.

Early on in their relationship, right when things were getting serious with Chris, she pumped the brakes. She told herself she wasn't ready and that she was going to get hurt. So, she looked for an escape hatch.

But that was just her self-protection mechanism activating itself: leave him before he can leave me. Afraid of getting too attached, she abruptly broke things off with him.

If you've ever felt the urge to pull away right when things are going well, started a fight just to feel close, or found some reason it wasn't going to work anyway, then you know exactly how these mechanisms work.

A week later, Chris surprised her.

Instead of closing the Jada chapter of his life, he did the opposite. He showed up at her door one morning, told her he was all in, and asked her to spend the rest of his life with him.

Stunned by Chris' proposal, Jada felt the flood of relief calm her nervous system. And it replaced any fear that made her push him away. With little hesitation, she said yes. But not before she made him promise to never leave her.

Chris said that would never happen. He told her he'd never loved someone so much. He told her that she was his queen.

Despite his outgoing personality—easily confused with flirtatious—Chris never cheated. He was too loyal for that. It never crossed his mind. What followed him instead was an underlying fear of conflict.

I was about to turn to Jada and ask, "What tells Chris that he's safe in this relationship?" when my mind hit pause. I couldn't help but watch Chris make a fist in one hand and cover it with his other. Back and forth. He kept repeating it—clenching, covering, unclenching—over and over.

He was clearly struggling. And it didn't take a behavioral psychologist to see it.

What Chris was doing with his hands spoke to me loud and clear: he was feeling unsafe. And in that moment, I really felt for the guy. Afraid of being judged poorly for who he was yet expected to remain calm despite the overwhelming emotions he felt.

Chris was in a double-bind. Feel, but not too much. Speak up, but only in a safe way. And whatever you do, don't trigger your spouse.

Chris was struggling to express himself without worrying that the conversation might turn unsafe. The result? He was conditioned to believe that sharing hard feelings can happen only if he's strapped in with a seatbelt and the airbags are in good working condition. What he's lost touch with is that hard conversations don't have to be anything more than just that: hard conversations. But if he interprets "I don't like what I'm hearing" as unsafe, the conversation will be just that—unsafe.

Case in point: when I asked him, "Chris, how would you describe your conversations with Jada?"

He replied, "Unsafe."

Are you seeing the double-bind? Here I am, needing to validate his characterizations of their conversations while also trying to convince him that tough conversations aren't necessarily unsafe and therefore worthy of avoiding. If we're going to get anywhere, I've got to help Chris gain the confidence to express himself while simultaneously not liking what he's hearing.

And I'm going to have to do that by meeting Chris where I know he needs to be met. So I circle back to Jada.

"We've got a big question to answer," I turned to her and said.

"How will Chris know that it's safe to speak his truth? To tell you everything and not leave out any little details, no matter how much you don't like to hear them?"

"I have no clue," she answered quickly. "If I did, we wouldn't be here right now!"

"I get that. But what if I told you that knowing how isn't the part that matters right now?" I replied. "There's something else we need to tackle first."

It's at this point in their story that I need to point out that these questions I'm asking Jada and Chris are meant to challenge their deepest fears.

Here are two people who love each other but are holding onto so much fear that they've convinced themselves that she's not stayable and he's not good enough.

The men in Jada's life, starting with her dad, sent her the message that she's not worthy enough to stick around for. And Chris' mother wasn't a saint either. She withheld love and approval when it suited her. Walking on eggshells became a life skill for Chris, training him to believe that other people's emotions were his responsibility.

Because of these wounds, Jada and Chris are locked into a vicious cycle of conflict, trying to get the message they both desperately want to hear. Jada constantly seeks reassurance from Chris that he isn't leaving. And Chris people-pleases or gets defensive whenever he feels attacked.

Like so many couples, both let fear dictate how they treat each other. And it's tragically ineffective.

You know what else is messed up? People are less afraid of checking their DMs while driving their 5,000-pound car at 90 mph than they are of talking to their partner about their innermost vulnerabilities.

If I could convince women that their husbands aren't leaving, and men that their wives like them despite their shortcomings, you'd think I could walk on water.

Here's how you cut through that.

"We've got to tackle fear first," I began.

"There's fear on both sides, you guys. Jada, you're afraid Chris is going to leave. And Chris, you're afraid to disappoint Jada."

"Right now, I can't teach you guys how to fight better," I told them. "I'd just be wasting our time because that's not going to take. Neither of you has a plan to defend your relationship against its biggest threat: your fears."

"When you're locked into a fight like what happened in the kitchen last Sunday, you're letting fear take over."

"Jada, for you it's that you're feeling leavable. And Chris, you're feeling like you're not allowed to disappoint her."

"And so you both automatically default into unconsciously asking the wrong question: how can I avoid my fear and the pain it brings?"

"Can you follow me so far?" I checked in.

Heads began to nod.

"In the heat of the moment, no one has the wherewithal to simply ask, 'How can we push aside our fear and ask for what we want?' That ultimately is reassurance. Reassurance that you're stayable. And reassurance that it's okay to tell the truth even if it means disappointing the other," I explained to them both.

I'm not naive enough to think it's easy to push past fear when you're fighting with your spouse. I don't have to look further than my own marriage to know how hard it is.

But I do know this: what makes fear so destructive is how efficient it is at shutting down curiosity when you're locked in a fight. It makes using hurtful words feel more natural than asking questions.

So let's zoom out and take an objective look at what happened the night Jada threw the plate that cut Chris above his eye.

We need to remember that they were two people who felt completely powerless in their ability to choose connection over fear.

I needed to help them get their agency back—and quickly. Here's how I did it.

"Guys, when we leave here today, I've got a simple exercise for you to do at home. I think we can all agree that if you knew how to let go of fear, you would have. And the fight on Sunday night would have gone vastly differently."

"But you didn't, and that's okay," I continued.

"Tonight, I want you to take a piece of paper. Personally, I like index cards. And on that paper, I want you to write: 'How can I trade fear for connection?' Then—and this is very important—you're going to read that to yourself daily."

Simply asking Jada and Chris to trade fear for connection isn't the magic bullet that's going to end their struggles. They won't be laying me off just yet; we've still got a lot of work to do. But it's where we have to start.

If they're going to rewire how they relate to each other, I need them to focus on what they want, not on what they don't want.

And this is why my process works in record-breaking time. Like Usain Bolt—only for your marriage.

Most therapists would take Jada and Chris down the path of over-analyzing why they're so afraid. Me? Forget that. I've got other clients waiting for me—and I don't have 52 weeks. I've given myself five. That's my deadline, not theirs.

I like Occam's razor: the idea that the simplest explanation is usually the correct one. Jada's dad and ex-husband both left her. That's why she's afraid of Chris leaving, too. Is digging up her past going to flip the switch and bring hope and optimism into her life? No.

And what about Chris' overbearing mother? Does bringing up his childhood wounds do anything but connect him to his pain? Will that remove any shame he feels for caring more about what others think than how Jada feels?

No. None of that will help them end their pain.

Chris and Jada want more connection and safety, and it's my job to help them build it. They don't need a better understanding of their pain. They live and breathe it every day.

Focusing on the problem may explain suffering, but it won't teach couples how to build a marriage that makes them feel chosen and cherished.

So, with Jada and Chris, we start by pushing fear aside. They're going to practice slowing down time, like Neo in *The Matrix*. I want them to see fear coming before it hits them. And when they do, they're to say, "Fear is not taking over this time. I choose connection."

"Wait a sec, Jonathan," I can hear you saying, "You didn't show them how to trade fear for connection!"

You're right. And I didn't have to.

By simply asking how you can get what you want—how to trade fear for connection—you trade fear for discipline. What sounds more appealing: carrying the weight of fear or of discipline?

Let's say it's Saturday night. You and your spouse are relaxing at home, watching a show on Netflix together, and one of you cracks a joke that comes across as sarcastic. Or insensitive. And that kicks off a fight between you.

Suppose one of you had the wherewithal to say, "Fear's not welcome here anymore," and ask, "How can I remind you that you're safe to disappoint me, and I'm not leaving because of it?"

Imagine what could be different if you were courageous enough to ask for what you want. Your night would probably go a lot better than my wedding night did.

Thankfully, my wife has more forgiveness than I have self-assuredness.

If I had known that simply asking for what I want was the best strategy, I'd have tattooed it on my forearm. That would've saved me from turning our special night into a traumatic core memory.

All I had to do was ask my wife, "Can you remind me I'm being an idiot to doubt you?"

Since most people don't come into my office to get tattoos, I suggest grabbing an index card instead and writing your version of the following:

"How can I trade fear for _____ (insert desire here) ______?"

I know this seems too simple. It's meant to.

Let me ask you this: What happens to fear when you wake up every day and make it your number-one mission to give your partner what they crave most from you?

When I presented this question to Jada and Chris, I let them sit with it for a moment.

"We're going to have to wrap up for today," I said, realizing my coffee had worn off.

"Oh, yes, I lost track of time," Jada responded. "Thank you, Jonathan. Feels like we finally have positive conversations to look forward to."

She didn't have to thank me. Watching her shoulders drop five minutes earlier was all the thanks I could've wanted. That told me I could feel confident about sending them home. That whatever conversations were waiting for them on the drive back would feel safer than the ones on the drive in.

We hadn't conquered conflict in that hour. But we had turned the volume way down on it.

Let's Pause Here...

You'll never get what you want in your relationship, if you can't see past your identity-level wounds.

"I'm not good enough."

"I'm not successful."

"I'm not wanted."

Words spoken like a true wounded warrior. I should know, because I spent the first 10 years of my marriage letting fear dictate how I treated my wife.

The real enemy in your relationship is fear.

It makes hurt people hurt people. Jada attacks to avoid abandonment. Chris hides to avoid conflict. Both are doing whatever they can to protect themselves but failing miserably at protecting each other.

"How can I avoid pain?" is the wrong question to ask.

The better question is: *"How can we trade fear for connection?"*

Why does that question work? Three reasons:

- It puts you on the same team.
- It names the thing every couple wants.
- It forces you to be curious.

In case you missed it, I'm intentionally asking you to be curious with each other. Why? Because curiosity leads to outcomes. Don't believe me? Then ask yourself:

"If we could make each other feel safe again, what would that mean to us?"

I know your answer will be: "Everything."

Chapter 7

Us vs. the Problem (Curiosity Builds a Team)

When Jada stepped over Chris' legs to sit down at the start of our second session, she almost fell in his lap. It would have been funny had you not seen the look of frustration on her face. Apparently, he couldn't be bothered to make room for her as she tried to take her seat. I could tell instantly that we'd backslid.

Damn, I thought, as I noticed that my watch was still on my wrist. I always take it off and put it on the coffee table before each session. I need to keep track of time and can't stand letting my clients see me check it—especially when I know the session is going to be a doozy.

When I can't keep track of the time, I risk not having enough of it to wrap things up and let them cool down. That means I'll be left scrambling trying to send them home feeling good enough to come back the following week.

"We couldn't be in a worse place," Jada said, reminding me of what she said when she kicked off our first session. "It feels like it's going to be this way forever."

"Of course you feel that way," I remarked. "That's what happens when we're stuck in the 'how-do-I-get-rid-of-my-emotional-pain' phase."

"How do we get off this train?" Jada followed with a question.

"Tell me what happened, and I'll help you," I said.

"I was trying to look for all the ways that Chris does things for me that make me feel secure," Jada began. "But then he goes and fucks it up. Last night, I walked into the bedroom and saw him on his phone again. He immediately closed down WhatsApp. Who's he talking to that he doesn't want me to see?"

"I wasn't talking to anyone!" Chris chimed in defensively. "And if I was, who the fuck cares? The only people I text with are my clients!"

Chris turned to me.

"What's the point?" he asked, expecting I'll throw him a lifeline.

But I don't. Even if I wanted to, it's not my job. Jada is the only one who can do that. I've got to let this cook. Their frustration has got to come out or there's no moving forward. You can't put joy back in if you don't let the pain out first. So I sat there and nodded.

"Sounds like a pretty gnarly fight," I reflected back at them.

"It's the same uphill battle," Jada said, with resignation in her tone. "We're never going to fix this."

"If you were open to hearing me, maybe we wouldn't be here," Chris tossed at her. "Every single time we get into these fights, all you do is accuse me of lying. Then you dangle divorce above my head like it's a piñata."

"All I do is pour love into you," Jada shared. "And every single time I do, you do stupid shit that you know makes me feel unsafe."

"I have to work! It's my job for Christ's sake," Chris pleaded. "Why won't you believe me? You're on guard all the time. You're constantly accusing me of doing God-knows-what behind your back no matter what I say. I'm not the one here who's broken!"

Now we're getting somewhere. We're not three minutes into this post-fight fight, and I can already tell you what's happening here.

Jada's struggling with her past. Correction: the trauma from her past.

Chris, on the other hand, has lost his peripheral vision. He's not understanding the meaning Jada attaches to his behavior, like shutting down apps when she walks in the room. He's got blinders on, and it's making it hard for him to see what's happening here.

Both of their emotions explode like firecrackers. They're both loud, colorful, and (un)impressive. They're trying to outcompete each other, and it's hard to listen to.

Jada's use of the word *divorce* isn't benign. It is a hurtful way of communicating how much pain she's in.

And there's irony in her choice of words. She's the one who feels the most unsafe, yet she reaches for the most destabilizing word possible. She does it for a reason: to make Chris feel her lack of safety. But whether she follows through or not, I will tell her that these threats need to go—and fast.

Meanwhile, Chris is walking close to the cliff's edge. His use of the word *broken* doesn't sit well with me. I understand that it's how he makes sense of her traumatic childhood. But he's not doing it in a good way. He's talking about who she is as a person and, unless you've got something good to say about your partner's identity, you'd better shut up.

By painting Jada with a broad stroke like this, it'll feel impossible for her to be anything but broken—in his mind and hers. I made a note to mention this to him later in the session.

Because of their pain, neither can see past their own worldview. Jada questions Chris' loyalty, and Chris questions Jada's ability to see him for the loyal man he is. There are no winners here. No wonder they feel hopeless.

"The reason your everyday stuff leads to big blow-ups," I began, "is because no one is pausing long enough to hear what the other person isn't saying."

"Isn't saying?" Chris asked.

"Yes, isn't saying," I repeated.

"When you guys are desperately trying to get the other to hear you, you stop speaking each other's language. That should clue you into the fact that you don't know who you're talking to."

"Want a loving and soft relationship?" I asked them both, without giving them time to answer.

"Then start by painting a portrait of your spouse in your mind. One you can be proud of. One you'd hang in the Louvre."

"The Louvre?" Chris again.

"Yes, The Louvre. If you can't see each other in a good light, you'll never get the one thing every couple roaming this good green Earth is searching for: sameness."

"Sameness?" Jada cocked her head to the side and queried.

"Yes, sameness. Not defined literally as the same—but one in spirit. As it's found in Mark 10 verse 8, two become one flesh."

"Oh, but we're not religious," Chris said.

"You don't need to be," I told them, "We're not here for that. But the Bible does have something important to teach us. Couples need to feel like they are on the same page. The same team. Like they are two people coming together as one."

I looked at Jada first.

"Take your mother-in-law, for example," I began. "How does it feel when Chris says she can fly out for the weekend and stay with you guys? And when those plans get made without asking you first?"

"I hate it," she said without hesitation.

"But he's being a good son, no? Shouldn't he have her back?"

"No," she blurted. "He should have my back first. Correction: not first. Only my back."

"So glad you made my case for me," I continued. "You're basically saying that no one, parents included, should come before your spouse. Is that your definition of loyalty? Your definition of a safe and connected relationship?"

"Yes, that's exactly my definition," she agreed.

"Well, Bible verse or not, I think we've established that sameness, as in being 'one,' is your dish of choice at the all-you-can-eat buffet, no?"

"Yes," agreed Jada and Chris.

"Wonderful. Now I think we can all agree that being one means being on the same team. So answer me this: why do NFL players all wear the same colorful jerseys?"

"They want to look like each other," offered Chris.

"Correct," I said.

"Another question for you: do these guys waste time thinking about whether they belong on the field or not? Or are they focused on making the next first down?"

"They're focused on the first down," Jada said as she lowered her head.

"Right again. If they're not trying to prove they belong on the team, then why are you trying to prove you belong in this relationship?"

I let that sink in before pressing them again.

"If you're questioning if your partner has what it takes to be in this relationship, you'll never feel like you're one."

Their silence told me the coin was dropping.

Jada and Chris spend too much time thinking the other needs to change, like the other is a project that needs to be fixed. And it's preventing them from seeing the biggest problem they have: a lack of curiosity.

The fallout?

No one bothers to ask: *"How can I show you that I trust you?"* or *"What could I do to help you trust me?"*

What's needed is a commitment to take each other at their word and figure out how to get on the same team.

Instead, they're arguing so loudly they may as well be wearing noise-canceling headphones.

Chris shuts down when Jada goes from 0 to 60. He looks for a corner to hide in, hoping the verbal assault will end soon. When deflection stops working, he tries defensiveness. And when that fails, he switches to the attack, like when he called Jada "broken."

Jada, on the other hand, doesn't trust a word coming out of Chris' mouth. Remember, her father left. So did her ex-husband. Those wounds weigh heavy on her heart. She can't help but escalate—her voice, her threats. She leads with big behavior but, on the inside, there's a wounded little girl who just wants to be loved. And committed to.

It makes complete sense that Jada and Chris can't have difficult conversations. They're trying to ride a bike for the first time without training wheels.

Just like Vanessa and Julian, there's too much pain here. It's sucking the life out of their relationship.

"Judging by how emotional things have been today," I said, pulling us back into session, "we're going to call a timeout and hit pause on the pain for a second."

"That would be great," Jada exhaled. "Every time we get into it, I feel like Chris has no space for me to share my feelings."

"I would, but you just come at me all the time with guns blazing," he said.

"See? He just reverses me," she countered. "Instead of addressing what I'm saying, he fires back at me for how I'm saying it. If he took a second to hear me and stopped trying to negate me, I wouldn't feel like he's putting me in a little box all the time."

"I'm not trying to put you in a box," Chris said. "But I've never once said I was going to leave."

"Then why do you always tell me you hate putting up with my shit?" Jada replied, tears falling into her lap. "I don't feel settled in this relationship because when I bring anything up, you shut down."

Jada's breathing started to accelerate.

"You tell me to calm down. Tell me to relax," she continued. "Well, I'm sorry. I can't relax. When your nose is buried in your phone talking with God knows who, how am I supposed to relax? It's not okay for some girl in your office to message you on a Sunday night! And I don't want your mother talking shit about me when I say no, she can't come for the weekend!"

"You see," Chris said, shooting a look of blame. "You said let's hit pause and here she goes, getting riled up again."

The temperature is indeed rising. No one ever said couples work was easy. Perhaps that's why many therapists avoid it.

"Maybe a timeout wasn't strong enough. Let's rewind the clock," I said, changing my approach. "What I see is an injured player on the field."

"Jada's hurt. And that triggers your defenses, Chris," I said, looking at him.

"If you want to treat an emotional injury, you have to meet her where she's at: on the emotional level."

I leaned forward.

"If she's not hearing you, it's because what you're saying isn't getting through. Most likely because you're speaking from your head—not your heart."

I paused and let that land.

"If you're playing defense while she's on offense, nothing you say will make sense to her. Sure, she'll hear the words you're saying, but they'll just confuse her."

I looked Chris in the eye, "Did you know her father left?"

"Yes."

"And her ex? You know he left, too, right?"

"I do."

"So I wouldn't be wrong to say you're aware of her insecurities?" I said, getting really personal here.

"No, you wouldn't," he admitted.

"Yet, you still chose her. You knew what she'd been through."

I turned to Jada. "And you didn't let it slip past you that Chris' mother left her own mark on him, right?"

"Yes, I am aware," she confessed.

"Well then, childhood wounds aside, I'll do my best to be fair and balanced and throw you both under the bus," I continued with a smile.

They both laughed.

"If you want to help, and let me stress *help*, each other work through past traumas, all you need is some patience and curiosity."

"How can we show that?" Chris struggled to ask.

"Easy!" I said with a little too much enthusiasm. "Just ask: 'how can I show you that we're on the same team?' No need to overcomplicate it."

"Or, if you want to get really proactive, instead of trying to prove your loyalty, you can do what I do: adopt the mission to wake up every day hell-bent on sending your spouse the message that they're safe, that you're here, and that you're not going anywhere."

"Would that move the needle some?" I asked.

Without waiting for an answer, I continued.

"I have a sneaking suspicion that it would. I want you to leave here today determined to play on the same team. Determined to remind each other that you're in this together. That's how you'll win."

"Can you do that?" I asked.

Chris was the first to stand up.

"I think we can," he said.

After they left my office, I sat back down and took a moment to admire them for how hard they were working. I wasn't totally convinced, but the smiles on their faces told me we'd regained some of the ground we'd lost.

My own smile told me there was hope they'd find an off-ramp for their pain.

Every couple suffers from pain, and it comes out as anger, frustration, tension, resentment—and the list goes on. That insight isn't going to win me any awards. But the understanding that pain shuts down your ability to be curious might.

It took me years to figure that out. And a few more to understand that the best kind of curiosity is bidirectional: curiosity for your partner *and* curiosity for yourself.

That means asking a ton of questions. And not the kind you type into Google, like, "How can I learn to fly a Cessna?"

The questions I'm talking about—the ones Jada and Chris should be asking—look like this:

"What would make you feel secure about my relationships at work?"
"How will you know—beyond any doubt—that I'm not going anywhere?"
"When do you feel like you can trust me?"
"What can I do to reassure you when you feel threatened?"
"How would you know that you're the only person that matters to me?"

These questions are just the start. They can be modified any way you like. And they are questions all of us can ask.

Couples need to remember: when pain starts calling the plays, "Am I with the right person?" is the wrong question to ask.

Doubling down on questions about compatibility will not do you any favors.

In fact, that'll only pour gasoline on the very conflict you're trying to resolve in the first place. You don't need to look further than Jada and Chris tossing around words like *divorce* and *broken* to understand that.

I've been married for 17 years, and I've come to learn this: your partner has a message they deeply crave to hear. And your questions are what tell them you understand what it is.

Case in point: my wife wants to know she's good enough.

Me? That I'm stayable.

For others, it's "I have your back," "You're a good man," or "You're chooseable."

All of us are used to sending messages to the people we love. In fact, most of us do it daily.

If you are a parent, there's a reason you tell your kids "I love you" over and over again, often 12 times before lunch. It's because you want them to grow up knowing that they're loveable. That they're safe. They matter. And you're there for them.

But your kids are still going to get hurt. Even under your watch.

It's not worth your time contemplating whether your kids will carry wounds into adulthood.

Without a doubt, they will.

But here's what'll make you sleep better: knowing that they picked a partner who was curious. Who wanted to sit with them, on the same team, and ask: How can I help you heal your wounds?

Jada and Chris didn't get the healthy parenting they deserved, like many of us. So they turned to each other for support. Unfortunately, the support they were looking for wasn't there.

What they need to understand is that it's not their job to heal each other's emotional wounds.

But playing the supporting role while the other does that work? Showing up with curiosity? Rejecting fear and reminding them you're not going anywhere?

Well, that's not an obligation—it's an honor.

And when you accept it, it'll turn your marriage into a deeply fulfilling one.

Let's Pause Here...

Too many good couples feel stuck. Not because they're overwhelmed with problems. But because no one stops to ask: "Do you want some help working through your past?"

Instead, they'd rather say, "That's not my job...go to therapy!"

You can't expect your partner to feel safe if you're unwilling to play a supporting role in their life and in healing the emotional wounds they walk around with.

It doesn't have to be hard. Questions like these don't have to be painful to ask:

"How will you know—beyond any doubt—that I'm not going anywhere?"

"What can I do to reassure you when you feel threatened?"

"How would you know that you're the only person who matters to me?"

Repairing after a fight takes a heck of a lot more energy than asking those questions ahead of time. And when you do, you'll soon discover: those fights become fewer and farther between.

And should conflict erupt, the work you've done will help you go from opponents to teammates so fast, it'll make your BFF jealous.

And if you really want to speed up that repair after a gnarly fight, pause and ask:

"How can we get through this together?"

Pain wants to break you. But curiosity? It'll build you.

That's the point of that question: to shift your focus from blame to togetherness.

What you want coming out of your mouth isn't "I need to fix you"; it's "How can I be with you in this?"

There you have it, two ways to loosen the grip conflict has on your connection: help them heal what hurts and stop seeing them as something to "fix."

Chapter 8

The Repair Cycle That Works (Turning Gunshots into Pinpricks)

"That's exactly what I said to him!" Jada blurted out. "We were having an incredible day. Just hanging out after the kids went to bed. And all I did was crack a joke."

"Sorry for being so sensitive!" Chris countered. "I've told you so many times that I don't like it when you compare me to my mother."

"Look, I know it feels like a gunshot wound," I interrupted. "But I think if you zoom out, you'll see that what we're dealing with is a pinprick."

Nearly every high-conflict couple I've worked with has a vision problem: they can't see the contra-evidence to their pain. Jada and Chris were no different. Just 15 minutes into our session, and all I'd gotten was a predictable stream of complaints.

"We need more tools," Chris turned to me and said. "Every time it feels like we're making progress, one of us gets hit with the next thing. It feels like shrapnel and that we're right back in the 'Spin Cycle.'"

"Ahh," I let out. "Good job, you guys, on externalizing the problem!"

In our last session, I had introduced Jada and Chris to the concept of "externalizing the problem." When they fought, they viewed their problems not as something they struggled against but as evidence that their relationship was broken. Or worse, that one of them was broken.

This is a common issue couples run into. They see conflict as a ticking time bomb: something catastrophic, not something they can overcome.

Why? Because they internalize it. They assume it's inherent to the relationship, not something the relationship can fight against.

Externalizing the problem is how you protect the relationship from the damage of conflict. Think of it like playing dodgeball on the same team, not tennis in a singles match. Instead of hitting problems back and forth, each partner helps the other get out of the way of oncoming balls.

You do that by recognizing your patterns, then giving these patterns (your cycle) a name, and finally working together to eliminate it or block it, like you would the opposing team.

So, to fulfill my promise of giving Jada and Chris tools for managing conflict, I had told them in the last session to give their fight cycle a name—preferably a silly, fantasy name that would be easy to remember. My wife and I used to call ours "Friday Night Fights." Back in the day, we'd come home on Friday after an exhausting week at work and, like clockwork, would get into a fight that would ruin our precious weekend together.

"I'm really glad to hear you took the homework assignment seriously," I praised them. "I know it doesn't eliminate conflict altogether, but did it help you see the other team winging balls past your head?"

"One hundred percent," Chris answered. "Thinking about conflict that way is definitely new for me. It made me feel like I'm fighting alongside Jada, not against her."

I couldn't help but stretch my smile ever wider at that moment. I book that as a win and remind myself to share it with Susan, my supervisor. She's always telling me to be more proud of my work, so I know she'll enjoy hearing the story.

"Really proud of you guys," I said, fighting back the urge to hug them. "And with that, let's get you some more of the tools you're looking for, Chris."

"That would be great."

"The way I see it, you've got two issues you're dealing with when you step onto a landmine," I began.

"First, you're not asking the right question: is this a pinprick or a gunshot we're dealing with? Both of you become overwhelmed with pain and lose perspective. You overtreat the injury, and that's a triage problem."

"Second, you're not maintaining composure. You're acting like aggrieved victims instead. You feel attacked and so you seek retribution—your pound of flesh. So you throw everything at each other, hoping something sticks."

"So, how do we get back on course?" Chris asked.

"Well, before I teach you that, we have to fix a vision problem," I replied. "Then we'll cover how to repair those pinpricks."

"Vision problem?" he repeated. "I'm not sure I understand."

"Right now, if some thoughtless gesture or comment is sending you to the ER, then it's not because an injury didn't happen. It's because you've lost interest in your partner."

"Whoa, how did we go from talking about a fight to all of a sudden not being interested in your partner?" Jada tagged herself in.

"We went there when the red flag waving above your heads mid-fight went unnoticed," I replied, as patiently as I could.

"Two people who are genuinely interested in their partner's lives are connected. But when that interest fades, so does connection, and fights like these become your default."

"Take curiosity," I continued. "Being interested in each other's life is the glue that holds two people together. The second you stop showing interest in how their day was, what their wins, struggles, and missteps were, you open the door for disconnection."

Chris smiled like he knew it was true.

"And when you stop sending the message that we're on the same team, you stop seeing each other," I said. "Then, every unkind tone of voice or insensitive comment feels like a stab wound. Like a gunshot. Pretty soon, each hurt blends into the next."

"Then, when shit gets really bad, you come see someone like me. And, for 50 minutes, you litigate your version of the truth—what he did last week, what she said that upset you."

"And so you don't hear the whole story," Chris said, catching my drift.

"Exactamundo," I replied. "Pain forces you to look for evidence that confirms your version of the truth. And the good stuff—effort, joy, and connection—you completely miss it."

As I shared this lesson with them, I was remembering a couple in their 40s I had worked with. He worked while she stayed home and homeschooled their kids. One day, overwhelmed, she couldn't find her wallet and so used his credit cards to pay for a delivery.

They shared accounts and had similar cards. Forgetting for a moment that she wasn't using hers, she entered the wrong PIN three times on each card and ended up getting both cards blocked.

If you want to know what frustration looks like, talk to this guy. He lived abroad with his wife and three kids, and suddenly the only working card left in his wallet was his platinum Amex.

Not a big deal—until both banks said resetting his PIN required visiting his home branch 3,000 miles away. Since he wasn't going back anytime soon, he was left relying on the only card half the world doesn't accept.

I told the story to Jada and Chris.

"I can't imagine how mad he must have been," Chris said, leaning forward, "What did he do?"

"He kissed his wife and thanked her for every single meal she made for them with all the groceries she bought for them as the only one of the two that saw the inside of a grocery store," I said with a smile on my face.

"And you know what made it possible for him to forgive her?"

"No, but I'd love to hear," Jada smiled.

"Because when he looked at her, he didn't see an absent-minded scatterbrain, as many would in that moment," I continued. "He saw a devoted mother and wife that knew no limits to the meaning of self-sacrifice. That's how."

I paused to let that sink in.

"In that moment, he had a choice: focus on her flaws or see the wonderful woman he was married to who, in a moment of absent-mindedness, made a mistake."

"Wow. I never thought of that before," Chris said. "I love that. How do you do more of that?"

"Glad to hear you ask that, Chris. Let me help you," I replied. "By choosing to see his wife for the self-sacrificing and extraordinary woman she is, he made her feel safe in an emotionally tense moment. But he could do that because he was interested in her. Interested in seeing her instead of her mistake."

Since I'd promised them tools, I then gave Jada and Chris these five conversation starters as homework.

They aren't silver bullets, and I warned them as such.

"These questions won't stop you from getting hurt, but they're what you need to build a bullet-proof vest for your relationship," I said. "They're meant to get you talking: about your hopes, dreams, and plans. The goal is to create the kind of connection that makes you look at each other in the heat of the moment and say, 'Yeah, we've got this.'"

"Are you ready?" I asked.

"Absolutely," he replied. "Hit us with them."

Here what I gave them:

1. *What's one memory from our relationship that makes you smile?*
   This question gets couples digging through their story to revisit nostalgia and connect with past wins. I start with the past to highlight their strengths as a couple.
2. *What could we have done differently in a recent fight to feel more heard or understood?*
   Everyone loves a redo. This question helps couples revisit conflict using curiosity and self-reflection—and it's trust-building gold.
3. *What's something you've been holding back that you wish I'd understand about our relationship?*
   This question creates space for a partner to share openly about how they're really feeling. It cultivates emotional connection now—not next week, not next month, now.
4. *If we could design our dream relationship, what would it look like?*
   Experience tells me that most couples love talking about the future. That's why I encourage them to create a shared vision and fill it with hope and optimism, two things essential for a healthy relationship.
5. *How can we become the best team we can be?*
   Great relationships are built by two people playing on the same team. This question invites both partners to tap into their individual strengths and use them for the common good.

"I like those questions," Chris said. "But how do you get through conflict without it feeling like you've been shot?"

"Patience, Chris," I replied. "We're getting there. You've got to know where you're going before you can get there."

"Fair enough. I just want to leave here with something."

"Don't worry. I'm not giving you a raincheck," I said. "You'll get the goods. Let me address one more thing about fear that I need to tell you."

"Right now, you guys are so wired for pain it feels like you're in an episode of Nagflix."

"Nagflix?" Jada laughed.

"Yeah, your new hit reality show. Enough complaining, bickering, and yelling to keep your audience glued to their screens. And you're doing it all: writing, directing, and acting."

Like great co-leads, they leaned in.

"And since you can't unsubscribe, every day feels like a new episode is going to drop. Even the slightest tone will wake up your nervous system."

Chris looked at Jada, "He's making sense."

"If you're under a microscope all the time, it's hard to stop playing your role—let alone quit the show."

"Oh my God!" Jada blurted out. "I couldn't have said that better. I always feel like if we're not perfect, we're broken."

"You guys were never broken. And neither was your relationship," I reassured her. "You're building perfection. Just like diamonds. Incredible beauty made under intense pressure."

"It just feels like we're both walking around, expecting the next fight to happen," Chris said.

"Of course it does. But don't be so hard on yourselves," I commanded. "It's time to give yourselves credit for fighting so hard for perfection."

"Not sure I'd call it that, personally," Jada chimed in. "Feels more like we're trying to hold a balloon under water."

"I can see that. But you're trying. And that counts for something," I did my best to reverse her.

"You know, Jada, we'd be in a much worse place if you didn't want to try in the first place. Am I wrong?"

"No, you're not," Jada admitted.

"Look, expecting the worst is only going to prime you for the worst. It invites fear and pain into your home."

I need to go slow here. They're going to need permission to lower their guard if they're going to stop their "Spin Cycle."

"When you see the 'Spin Cycle' coming, tell yourselves to trade it for the repair cycle I'm about to teach you."

This is a pivotal moment.

They have to decide if they're ready for something new. If they don't believe they can do it, they won't.

If self-doubt hijacks their confidence, they'll pull each other back into their Spin Cycle.

I look at them both.

"Are you ready to give this your all?"

"Absolutely!" Chris exclaimed.

"100%. I'm all in!" Jada said, committing.

"Here's what you're going to do. Don't be afraid of conflict. It's like a balloon: you can't hold it under water forever. It's going to surface no matter what. So give yourselves permission to let the fight happen. If it's going to anyway, a little 'who cares' helps."

They both looked surprised.

"Next, focus on three things: pause, reconnect, and repair."

"Pause, reconnect, repair. Are we supposed to commit that to memory?" Jada asked, a hint of sarcasm in her tone.

I ignored it. "Exactly. Just what I was about to tell you to do. When couples go about their day, they have a plan—a plan for a happy life. And it's a beautiful one. The problem is that the plan falls apart the second someone gets upset. In that moment, they lose access to the words that helped you write the plan in the first place. So I want you to commit that repair sequence to memory. It's going to help you say what actually matters most: *'I'm sorry for how I hurt you.'*"

Jada and Chris looked at me like their eyes were going to pop out of their sockets.

"Are you saying we have to say 'sorry'?" Jada asked.

"That's exactly what I'm saying. And you may have to say it more than once—until your partner believes you."

"What if I'm not sorry?" she asked.

"Before you call me crazy, let me remind you: we're talking about your partner. You know, the one you chose."

"Uh-huh, I remember," Jada said, nodding.

"So when they're hurting, you need to help them. Clearly. But conflict makes it really hard to know what to say and how to say it. That's why, at the start, words don't land."

"Crawl before you walk," Chris said.

"Yes, Chris—exactly!" I said. "Trying to talk it out creates friction. That is why it'll likely fail. You're skipping two crucial steps: pause, and reconnect."

"It sounds counterintuitive, though," Chris said, questioning me.

"I know, but hear me out. There's no getting to the repair step without the both of you feeling 100% ready. And you won't feel ready if you've got a ton of adrenaline and cortisol pumping through your veins."

Their frowns faded a little, so I continued.

"To kick off the repair cycle, one of you has to reach for the smelling salts. What does that look like? That's calling out the name you've given your cycle. That would sound like, *'Watch out! The Spin Cycle is starting!'*"

They both smiled again.

"After calling out the name of your fights, your focus turns toward the first step, which is to pause. Say something like, 'Sweetheart, the Spin Cycle is starting. I think we need to hit pause on the control panel. Can we take a second to catch our breath?'"

Jada giggled.

"The pause is your intermission. It's what gives your nervous system time to blink and reset. You might only need a few seconds or a few minutes. But if you want to take an hour—or pick it up after dinner—that's fine, too. Right now, the only focus should be on delay, until you're both regulated again."

"Delay? I can't do that," Jada said, protesting now.

"Yes, delay. You've got to delay. You won't have the brake pads to stop the fight in the moment."

I paused to catch my breath.

"I don't hate that idea," Chris said, giving Jada a glance.

"Trust me, that delay will give your brain the time it needs to resolve your fight. Although I have a sneaking suspicion that you won't want to."

Jada crossed her arms. "Are you saying we won't want to resolve the fight?"

"That's right," I answered her.

They looked at me, incredulous, so I explained further.

"If you've paused long enough to catch your breath and call out the cycle, then you're ready for step 2."

I paused, demonstrating what I meant.

"Step 2 is where the magic happens. You physically reconnect. Remember all that adrenaline and cortisol pumping through your veins? That's your nervous system out of whack."

"What do you do then?" Chris asked.

"You reset—physiologically. Think of it like a weighted blanket. You're using any physical gesture to signal, 'You're safe with me.'"

"So, in the middle of the fight, should I touch her elbow or something?" Chris asked.

"Yes, that's exactly what I mean," I replied. "You don't even have to touch them. It can be as simple as sitting down or relaxing your shoulders. Anything that sends the message you're no longer operating at DEFCON 1."

Chris shifted back in his seat, picking up on the signal.

"For some people, physical touch is too much. They may not be ready for that. In that case, I'd suggest downshifting. So read the room. Check in with each other. Maybe you just need to relax your shoulders or make soft eye contact."

"If you need help figuring out what to do, ask yourselves: 'What could we do to reconnect?'"

"Remember last session, Chris? Let curiosity be your guide. Is that asking, 'Can I get you a glass of water?' or 'Should I sit down instead of standing over you?'"

"I like that," he said.

They seemed ready for step 3, the repair.

I love this part—because it's the easiest of them all. It's a simple script that'll allow you to hit five emotional targets:

1. *"Sweetheart, I hurt you and hate that I did."*
   Here's where you take ownership. Resist the urge to justify or minimize. It's in this moment you let them know that what you did wasn't okay.
2. *"I don't want to fight with you. I want to fight for you."*
   This is how you signal that you're ready to get back on the same team.
3. *"I care more about you than being right."*
   Dropping your pride—as hard as it is—is how you let them know you choose your relationship over everything else.
4. *"I see your pain, and I'm willing to be a container for it."*
   When you find yourself in a hard conversation with your partner, remember: they need your presence, not your withdrawal.

5. *"I still choose you, even when it's hard."*
   Conflict tests commitment, so show them you're committed.

Chris pulled out his phone. "I like that," he said, typing enthusiastically.

Jada nodded at me. She believed him.

"Before we wrap up for the day," I started to say, but Jada interrupted.

"Oh, wow, that went fast."

"Take that as a good sign. It means we got a lot done. Had we sat in silence, I'd have wondered where the love had gone."

Jada smiled at Chris. He squeezed her hand.

"I was about to say, when it comes to repairing conflict, you don't need the perfect words. You just need the courage to put your pain on hold. I know it's not easy, but when you put reconnection first, you'll find out that the little hurts start to feel no worse than hitting a small pothole."

"So remember the repair cycle," I said. "And should your 'Spin Cycle' randomly turn on, respond with 'Pause, Reconnect, Repair.'"

"Appreciate the reminder," Chris said. "We'll see you next week."

Let's Pause Here...

My wife and I used to have drag-out fights that would last for days. Our struggle wasn't with the actual hurt we caused each other. It was with the exaggerated pain we felt from it.

Arguing with your spouse always feels worse than it really is because we see their behavior as an attack on our identity. That is how we personalize the pain.

And when your identity feels attacked, your connection begins to decay.

So what do most couples do when they find themselves in conflict? They try to talk their way out it. And they fail—or take a long freaking time to do it.

What they should be focusing on is building safety first. By safety, I mean physically and emotionally. That's where the pause, reconnect, and repair sequence comes into play.

First, hit pause. Give your nervous systems time to settle.

Second, reconnect physically to bring your heart rate back under control.

Then you're ready for repair. That's when simple scripts like "*I'm sorry for how I hurt you*" finally land.

This takes perseverance—especially if you're the only one doing it.

But if you lead by example, and rinse and repeat until it comes naturally, you'll be proof that repair doesn't need perfect words.

It simply needs practice.

Chapter 9

Take the Armor Off (Speaking the Truth That Scares You)

"How are we doing?" I asked, practically suffocating from the tension in the room. Chris' flexed jaw told me everything I needed to know. This wasn't going to be pretty. But the heck with it, I thought. If this balloon is going to pop, I may as well put the pin in it. At least we'll have 55 minutes to send these guys home feeling better than when they got here.

"We're coming off a gnarly fight," Jada answered, since Chris' jaw wasn't working.

"I'm sorry to hear that," I replied. "Tell me what happened so we can navigate out of this together."

"I'm really struggling right now, because if I hear the word *divorce* again, I'm going to lose my mind," Chris chimed in.

I ignored Chris' revelation, making a note to address it later. I can only tackle one thing at a time, and I assumed, correctly, that Jada's threat came off the heels of a different hurt. A hurt that kicked the gnarliness off in the first place.

"He deleted another message," Jada let out. "We were driving to Lincoln's baseball game. That's our eldest. I used Chris' phone to check the traffic and a message popped up."

"Our eldest," I thought. Interesting choice of language. I'd normally ask about that, since the boys were born to a different dad. But I'd wait. This was clearly a sign there were protective factors in their relationship. I put it in my session notes, planning to circle back to this noteworthy point when we'd start the repair process in 15 minutes or so.

"It was Kendra. His 'work wife,'" Jada sneered.

"Work wife?" I asked, stunned at her characterization.

"Yeah, I know. She's even joked about that with Chris. I don't like it, and I don't like her."

"That's not okay," I said, reassuring her. "I wouldn't be okay with that either."

"She works in his office. I've never liked her lack of boundaries, so every time I see a message from her, I can't help myself, and I read it. That's when I saw he deleted one of her messages. I've asked him a million times why he does it, and he just shrugs me off."

Chris sat there shaking his head, looking like a defendant in an orange jumpsuit as the judge read out the charges.

"Why do you *think* I delete messages?" Chris blurted out.

"I don't know!" Jada cried. "But I'm sure she does! What else does she know about us that you're too afraid to tell me?"

"I don't know. Maybe that you've lost your mind?!" Chris shot back. "That you're threatened by everyone? I can't tell you how embarrassing it is every time you call and we get into a fight. I can feel the entire office staring at me."

"Do you hear how he talks to me?" Jada turned to me, looking for a lifeline.

"I hear a lot of harsh words being spoken here," I affirmed. "But that's nothing compared to the pain I see."

"But if I'm being honest, Jada," I said, having decided to push further, "I'm glad Chris brought up the word *threatened* because I'm not entirely convinced that word is reserved exclusively for you."

"Right? Exactly!" Jada sighed, this time grabbing the lifeline.

"There's a lot going on here. For both of you," I swiveled my head back in Chris' direction. "I think now is a good time to hit that pause button I told you about last week."

"While you guys are locked in a debate about who hurts more," I pressed on, "Neither of you stops long enough to say, 'I see you're scared. I'm sorry you're feeling that. Let's put our armor down and talk about it.' You don't because you can't. Because, if I'm frank, you're both acting out of fear. You're both too afraid to tell each other what's really going on for you."

"I don't know how to stop," Chris said, dropping his chin. "The yelling, the screaming, the accusing. It feels hopeless. She can't use a filter. Couldn't find one if she looked, in fact. The second she starts swearing at me, I transport to another dimension. I check out."

"I have a filter," Jada protested. "You just don't see it. The minute I bring anything up, you go straight into defensive mode. Your eyes gloss over, and you get a look on your face like you're completely shell-shocked."

"That's because I am! You wear me down so much, I can't hear a thing that you're saying when you're so angry."

"But I don't start that way," Jada said, protesting again. "You just think I do. Every time I come to you with anything, it's always, 'here we go again.' You make me feel like I'm a nutcase. You roll your eyes. Stop listening. And walk away from me."

"That's because you just want to argue. And I'm done with it. If you want to discuss something, then discuss it. But if you want to shout at me, I'm the wrong guy for that."

"There's no other way to get you to hear!"

"If you're so good at hearing, then why don't you believe me when I say those messages are no big deal?"

"Well, if they're no big deal, then why do you delete them? What are you afraid to admit?"

"I'm not afraid of anything. Because nothing's happening!" Chris said, throwing his hands up. "The only thing that's going on is you married a salesman. I'm in sales, remember? I sell tech. To people. And I sell a lot of it because people want to buy from people they like."

Chris looked at me. "Dear God, it's my job! This is the same argument that happens every day that blows up in my face."

"The problem is not that the argument is the same," I challenged. "It's that neither of you is digging deeper. You're stuck scraping the surface. If you don't lean into pain with courage, you're going to run from it instead. Like two wounded children."

"Scraping the surface?" Chris queried.

"Yes. On the surface, you've got anger and resentment. That's the tip of the iceberg. But underneath that, you've got pain that's big enough to sink the Titanic. You guys are coming in guns blazing. But really, you're both scared."

I turned to Jada. "What does it do to you when you see a deleted message? Or Chris gets a text after hours? What's the fear you're feeling?"

She took a deep breath. "That he's gonna leave."

I turned to Chris again. "And when she's coming in hot? What are you feeling?"

"That I'm in trouble. That I'm not good enough," he answered, eyes staring at his feet.

"Good. Now we're getting somewhere."

"What about this work text from Kendra on a Sunday," I said, still looking at Chris. "Is there a fire at work you need to put out or is that random chit-chat?"

"Chit-chat, I suppose."

"Ordinarily, I'd say that isn't a big deal," I began. "But the topic of Kendra is clearly a touchy one. Have you guys talked about texting with co-workers? Is it on the menu for you guys if it happens after-hours or about non-work-related stuff?"

"No. I mean, yes, we've talked about it. And no, it's not on the menu. Jada has said it makes her uncomfortable."

"So maybe it would be a good idea to figure that out today," I continued. "Would that be reasonable? Does that sound like something you can do?"

"I guess so."

"If it's urgent, tell her it's okay to message you. Otherwise, can you tell her to put whatever she has to say in an email?" I asked, catching Jada's head nodding out of the corner of my eye.

"I can do that."

"And whether you said it, or Kendra did, I don't think it sends a very reassuring message if she's referred to as your 'work wife,'" I couldn't let that earlier disclosure slip through the cracks.

"I get that it's just a joke at this point. But that's not protecting your marriage," I continued. "It's your job to send everyone the message that your wife and family get your inner circle time, not your co-workers. Can you get on board with that?" I asked Chris pointedly.

"Yes. Of course, yes," he replied. "For the record, I never called her that. Kendra refers to herself that way."

"Then it sounds like another opportunity to tell her it makes you feel uncomfortable when she does."

Chris looked at Jada, "I will tell her that it makes me uncomfortable. I'm sorry she calls herself that. And I'm sorry I didn't acknowledge how it hurts you."

"When you see a notification go off on Chris' phone, Jada, there are two ways to communicate with him. You can ask for transparency or proof of innocence."

Jada nodded sheepishly.

"No one feels good about being tested all the time. And I don't think it's doing you any good to lead with the presumption of guilt."

"It's not. You're absolutely right," she replied.

"There's nothing wrong with leaning into your fear," I said reassuringly. "You can simply ask Chris to tell you what the message was. And ask for reassurance that he's still here. Just pause when you do so you give him the chance to answer."

Chris let out a sigh of relief. "I'd be happy to! I want to do that."

"And if you have the urge to delete something, don't," I turned back to Chris.

"If you're scared that a message is going to hurt her, don't fix it by hiding it. Fix it by narrating it. Let her in on the story."

Jada nodded again, faster.

"You guys need to start saying 'the thing under the thing,'" I continued. "That's the conversation hiding underneath all your pain."

"Jada, you're going to say: 'I'm afraid you'll leave.' And Chris, yours is: 'I'm afraid I'm not good enough.' It's time to put those two sentences in the room before you put the gloves on."

Chris reached over and put his hand on Jada's knee—their first contact all session. "Okay, I can say that."

"Good." I leaned back. "We're not interested in who punched harder in round 1, 2, or 12. You need to change the sport. And you do that by asking for the reassurance you both want."

Moments like this remind me: therapy isn't about reconstructing timelines or laying charges against the perpetrator. We're here to name the wound and interrupt the cycle that keeps the conflict going.

Who's more hurt is irrelevant. How we treat the wound is what matters.

Almost on cue, Chris took a sip of water and asked, "How do you work with two people coming from such different backgrounds?"

"Do you mean that one of you comes from Mars and the other Venus?" I said in jest.

"I just meant," he continued, "from a family-culture perspective. What do you do with completely different expectations? We're so different. If she's always seeking reassurance and I'm exhausted all the time, how does this not result in constant battles in our marriage?"

"I'm pretty sure you're asking the wrong question, Chris," I replied. "The last time I checked, if you cool steam, it turns to water. Heat ice, and it turns to water. Either way, you're both made of the same thing: water."

That's the part Jada and Chris were missing.

"It doesn't matter where you start. The thing that matters most is what you both want," I continued. "Right now, what you're both failing to see is that the most beautiful thing about people is intangible. It's their mind. And so, there are no differences between you two."

"You both want to be loved, no? Maybe even to feel chosen and cherished?"

Jada and Chris looked at each other and smiled.

"I'm not staring at two people with polar opposite backgrounds. I'm looking at two people that crave love, acceptance, safety, and security. The problem is that you've got scripts running in your head about why things are hard between you."

"Scripts? What scripts?" Jada inquired.

"Scripts like you're leavable, Jada. That script."

"Oh, yeah," she said. "You're right about that."

"And how you talk about Chris makes me think you define him by what he says or does."

Chris perked up with that one.

"But these scripts aren't true. Would you call your son a bad boy for hitting his friend at school? Can someone be 'leavable' because their crack-addicted father like mine left when I was four?"

That personal disclosure woke them up.

I shared it because they need to understand this: by buying into your own negative narratives, you're not doing yourselves any favors.

"Jada, when you see Chris get a text late on a Sunday, you automatically think: Who's that? Are they a threat? Is he going to leave?"

I turned toward Chris.

"And Chris, instead of thinking, 'Oh, no. I messed up. Let me fix it,' you go straight to, 'I'm messed up, and now you won't love me anymore.'"

"Hold on a second," Chris jumped in. "How am I messing up when someone from work texts me? I didn't initiate anything."

"Let me reverse you, if I may. You said it's not easy for you to be clear with co-workers about what you're comfortable with, right?"

"Uhh, yeah," he admitted.

"So you're going to get all kinds of messages from them—Kendra included."

"Uh-huh."

"And what's in those messages? Is she discussing a client? Sending you memes? What?" I asked.

"She, uh," he was slow to answer. "She was asking about my weekend."

"My case in point. What you've got is a loose boundary," I started to explain. "It's not a gross breach of trust, but for someone whose wife is not okay with it, that might not be a boundary worth ignoring."

It was clear Chris felt safer walking on eggshells than telling the truth.

"What Jada needs to feel safe in this relationship is a man that not only sticks around but sticks his neck out no matter how much it'll sting."

I have words for Jada about the flip side.

"And Jada, when you're married to someone who struggles with disappointing others, it helps to remind them that they can do something wrong, but that doesn't make them a bad person."

"What? So it's my job to prop up Chris' ego?" Jada fired back.

"Only if you care that he has a healthy one," I quipped.

I took a sip of coffee to let that sink in.

Here's what that means for their relationship: Jada and Chris were conditioned to believe they couldn't change how they attach to each other.

There was a good reason for that.

Years after her father moved out, Jada ran into him in a shop near her house. She hadn't spoken to him in more than a year. He'd driven an hour to pick up a gift for his girlfriend but never called his daughter to suggest meeting up. That hurt her—a lot.

Chris' mother was no less hurtful. One minute she was angry, the next she was soft. No matter what mood she was in, Chris was always responsible for it.

Jada and Chris learned that curiosity and safety could be replaced with indifference and impatience. That left a mark. When they're hurt, instead of offering connection, they lead with, "*Why should I give you anything? You hurt me.*"

So, their pleas to be seen the way they want—Jada, that she's stayable, and Chris, that he's good enough—fall on deaf ears. Neither of them is self-aware enough to ask, "*How can I give you the reassurance you crave?*"

What's worse is there's no urgency to help the other heal.

So I came back to them with a thought experiment:

"If you saw one of your kids laying beside their bike at the end of your driveway, wouldn't your first instinct be to run over to them, pick them up, and tell them they'll be okay?"

They both nodded.

"That's what needs to happen here. When you see that the other one is hurt, go to them and say: 'I see you. You're scared. Scared I'll leave. Scared you're not good enough.' That is the moment to make them feel safe. To show them you see the fear that lies beneath the surface."

"And how do you do that?" Jada asked.

"With curiosity," I replied. "What would it mean to Chris if you asked him, 'How can I show you that I'm here and that I want to help undo that message you've held onto for so long?'"

Chris looked at Jada, and she smiled. I relaxed a little—they were seeing each other.

Here's what most couples miss when they're in pain.

Chris and Jada don't have a choice when it comes to helping heal the other's wounds. They signed up for that when they said, "I do." Sure, they could protest. But if growing old together is what they want, they have to do it.

"Help heal their wounds?" I hear you asking.

Yes, help them.

It's not your job to heal your partner. That's their job. But wouldn't it be nice if they had your help?

Wouldn't it be good for your relationship if you helped close the emotional gap that separates you?

I think we can all agree it would be.

Here are two steps to help you do that. They're designed to separate your partner's pain from their identity, and help you get what you actually want, without putting them on the back foot.

First, establish safety around each of your starting points. Talk about what hurts but in a way that focuses on the problem, not the person.

One partner might say, "When you get frustrated with me, I sometimes feel like it's a criticism of who I am."

The other could respond, "That's not how I see it. I'm just reacting to the situation or behavior."

This helps create the safety you need for open communication.

Second, have a conversation that's focused on how you will move forward together.

Use these questions to talk about unmet wants and desires—without turning them into an attack:

1. *"When do I feel safe asking for what I want?"*
2. *"How can we make it easier to ask for what we want?"*
3. *"How will I know that I'm ready to hear what my partner really wants?"*
4. *"What would it mean to us if we felt safe to share our deepest desires?"*
5. *"How can we talk about what's not working without it feeling like an attack?"*

I know that getting what you want is easier said than done. Conflict makes it hard to not feel like it's their fault when you're hurt.

But you know what else is hard?

Growing up without your father in your life, like Jada's two boys.

How does that have anything to do with building safety during conflict?

Well, Jada and Chris were forced to navigate a challenging family dynamic when they blended their two families. I'm not a parenting expert, but I can tell you they did something right. They aligned on something that matters a lot to children: they built a safe and loving home for them.

Recall the way Jada said, "our son"?

I didn't see any hesitation on Chris' face when she said it. He was all in.

That tells me that when messages matter, they have the words to send the right one.

I didn't miss my chance to point it out.

"Jada, when you said, 'our son,' that mattered. A lot."

"Yes, they're ours. All of them are ours. We make no distinction around biological parents," she clarified.

"I love that," I commended her. "Since you guys are good at reminding your kids they're lovable, that should be an easy message to send each other."

"Well, since you put it that way," Chris said, reaching for her knee again. "I'm ready to try."

"Me, too," Jada cracked a smile when she looked at Chris.

"Good. Now I want you to keep doing what you've done here today. Before the volume rises, you're going to say the thing under the thing. Jada, say to Chris: 'I'm afraid you'll leave.' Chris, say to Jada: 'I'm afraid I'm not good enough.'"

"We can do that," they said almost in unison.

"Just remember, words are great—but they're not enough. You have to follow up with behavior. Chris, that means no deleting. Tell Jada what's going on in your world. And set boundaries at work: if it's urgent, call me. If not, put it in an email."

Chris nodded, "I can do that."

"Jada, you've got to help Chris out a little. Ask him for transparency, not proof of innocence. A simple 'Tell me what that message was about' will do. Then give him a second to answer. He deserves your faith in him. He's here now. If he was going anywhere, he wouldn't be."

"He does deserve my faith in him." Jada smiled again.

"Great! This is the progress we're looking for."

Repair never comes from winning the fight. It comes from naming what's underneath—and leaning into that with vulnerability.

"When you slow down and name your pain, you can do something about it," I said. "And one more thing for the road. When you find yourself neck-deep in an argument, remember it's just fear trying to take over."

"Fear's trying to make you dance the 'protest polka.'"

"That's what my old supervisor used to call it when two people were stepping on each other's toes trying to be heard."

"The protest polka," Chris laughed. "I like it."

"Yeah, it's catchy," I agreed. "So, the next time you're flooded, resist the temptation to pick at old wounds. That only makes them take longer to heal. When you want to soften, simply say, 'I'm afraid you'll leave me… judge me…hurt me.'"

Vulnerability is scary, but with practice, Jada and Chris will start saying things like, "I'm sorry for the message I sent you. That's not how I want you to feel."

Jada looked at Chris and smiled.

"I love you," he said, returning the smile. "And I'm sorry this is so hard. But let's do this—for us."

"Just know that none of these words are magic. But they're a doorway. Walk through it together, and you can stop dancing the protest polka."

"I think I speak for us both when I say there's nothing we want to do more," Jada confirmed.

As our session came to an end, I couldn't help but think of my wife.

She still struggles to believe she's good enough. And me? I still need reminding she's not going anywhere.

Our marriage isn't perfect—but we still sleep well at night.

Our commitment to showing up, repairing, and reminding each other that "You're not doing this alone" is never going away.

"Next session," I tell them, "I'll show you how to replace your anger with an apology that sticks."

Chris rose to his feet and held out his hand for Jada.

"I can't wait."

Let's Pause Here...

I'm not afraid of my wife getting upset with me. That's because the pain above the surface is never as scary as what's underneath it.

Fighting well means having the courage to say the thing under the thing.

If you remember, my wife's always working on saying, "I'm afraid I'm not good enough to be loved."

And me? "I'm scared you'll leave because I'm not stayable."

Those are identity-level wounds that conflict is always trying to hide.

For you and your partner, those wounds may be different.

Since you've chosen to be together, it is worth finding out what they are.

Speaking from experience, they will always be a part of your relationship. But if you respond to them enough with courage and vulnerability, they won't feel so intimidating anymore.

If you keep critiquing your partner's behavior instead of protecting their identity, you'll stay stuck in conflict, not connection.

You can't fix what you don't look for. And you can't heal what you don't find.

So ask, "*What did you grow up believing about yourself that still hurts today?*"

And when they tell you, respond with, "*I'd love to help you heal that. Would you let me try?*"

Just two simple questions, meant to disarm and replace fear with connection.

Now if they have trouble answering, or shut you down when you ask, downshift and go slower.

A simple "*What would it mean to you if you felt safe to ask for what you want?*"

I work with a lot of folks whose partner struggles to tell them what they want.

And to them I say, "Give them what they don't know they want—reassurance—and they'll tell you what they do want next."

Chapter 10

Go First and Win (the Clean Apology That Actually Lands)

The room felt lighter the moment Jada and Chris sat down.

"I usually don't pick up on good energy unless a couple has just been intimate after a long hiatus," I opened. "But knowing you guys, that was never an issue."

If sex wasn't responsible for their good mood, something else deserved the credit.

"We're having a really great week," Jada started.

"We *were* having a great week," Chris corrected her. "Until last night."

"Yeah, sure, last night wasn't great," Jada said with a slight smile on her face. "But one tough moment doesn't mean we need to rewrite the entire week. We actually had a great week!"

"I love that!" I cheered, making sure to congratulate them. "This is a big deal. I don't think I've heard the words *great* and *week* in the same sentence coming from either of you."

This vibe is too positive not to dissect. "So, give me the goods. How did you guys work through last night?"

"We'd finished dinner, and I brought up the homework you gave us," Jada began.

"Yeah, she always knows when to lay into me," Chris said with a chuckle. Good. The mood was still light.

"That's when she asked when I was going to speak to Kendra," Chris continued.

"That was also when you left the table," Jada looked at me and said. "I just wish I could share my feelings without him retreating."

"Thanks for sharing that, Jada. I think there's something we need to address before we talk about the Kendra bit." I chose my next words carefully to avoid implying that Chris was avoidant.

"Chris, I know your first instinct is to duck and run for cover, but something tells me it's how Jada starts the conversation that gets you tripped up."

"Yes, a thousand percent," Chris confessed.

He looked like a man who felt understood.

"But hang in there a second," I said to slow him down. "This isn't about throwing Jada under the bus for how she talks to you. I'm pretty sure everyone's communication could use improvement around here."

"Fair enough," he said, reluctantly. "It would just be great if we could make that happen."

"Let's do that, then" I said. "Starting with lesson number one: your overuse of the word *just*."

"Come again?" Chris' eyebrows pinched together. "What's wrong with saying *just*?"

"Good question," I said. "Let's focus on what was said: 'I just wish I could share my feelings without him retreating.' 'It would just be great if we could make that happen.' Do you guys remember saying that?"

"Yeah," he answered.

"Good. Now, don't take this the wrong way, but using that word makes communication feel exhausting. And it ruins any chance of talking without one of you getting defensive."

"How's that?" Jada looked puzzled.

"Because it raises the emotional stakes too much. 'Just' is almost never neutral—it signals something loaded is coming next."

Jada and Chris exchanged looks like I'd lost the plot.

"'Just' is a bargaining word you use when you expect to be denied. But it takes a clean request and wraps it in friction. You're escalating your wants to increase your chances of getting them."

"Like what?" Chris asked.

"Like, 'I just want you to listen' or 'Can you just help me?' It sounds like you're minimizing your request, but you're actually escalating it."

They still looked confused.

"It's the same issue with the word 'need.' As in, 'I need you to hear me.' What you mean is 'I've asked for this before, and since I'm not getting what I want, I'm making it sound more urgent.'"

When I hear the words "just" or "need," I know someone's feeling spent. And if both partners are throwing out those words, I know they're in need of serious reconnection work.

I have to teach Jada and Chris a cleaner way of asking for what they want—and that starts with dropping emotional-fillers like *just* and *need* from their conversations.

I also want them to respond with: "How can I help you get what you want?"

I'm not an English teacher anymore—haven't been since that job I had in Tokyo in my 20s. But I've come to understand how much language matters.

Too many people discount the power language has, both for good and for bad. If they took the time to understand it, they'd realize that *just* is neither safe nor simple. It's emotional resignation. Once you understand that, you stop pleading and start connecting.

Chris leaned forward.

"It never occurred to me what our choice of words meant," Chris said. "I just relied on my favorite tactic: 'avoid 'til go away.'"

"See!" I blurted out. "You're using it again!"

"I surrender, Jonathan. You got me," he laughed.

Jada didn't pick up on our playful tone.

"Well, I still feel exhausted asking for what I want—no matter how I ask," Jada said. "It never feels like he truly wants to help me."

"Can you blame me?" Chris scoffed. "Every time she brings something up, it feels like an attack—not a conversation."

"Wait a second," I interrupted. "When you guys sat down, I was feeling really good. Call me a plant, but the energy I was picking up felt good."

"Yeah, sorry," Chris apologized.

"Nothing to be sorry about," I corrected him. "I want you walking out of here feeling better than when you came in."

"That means a lot," Jada said. "This is hard, but we need this."

I sighed. "Good. I'm glad that it's helpful—not that it's hard."

"Let me continue, because it only gets better," Jada said with a hint of sarcasm. "I asked him when he was going to talk to Kendra. He said he hadn't thought about it yet."

"That's right and wrong," Chris replied. "I'd thought about it. But I was struggling to figure out what I was going to say to her."

"Which really hurt my feelings," Jada added. "Because all I wanted was for him to look at me and tell me when he's going to do it."

"Makes perfect sense," I affirmed.

"All I wanted was a timeline. I wasn't asking for much," she continued. "I want to know that he's open to hearing how it hurts me and that he'll set the boundary with her."

"I will. And I do hear you," Chris pleaded. "But this is new for me. Remember, I've been working with Kendra for a long time. It's uncomfortable. That doesn't mean I'm not going to do it. I just need a little more time."

"To work up the courage," I finished his sentence in my head.

Jada looked at Chris. "I understand that. But I want you to want to do it. Not because you're afraid of a fight. But because it matters to you. Because I matter to you."

Jada is right about that.

Chris needs to take the lead here. That means confronting Kendra regardless of how awkward the conversation will be.

Friendships that work when you're single don't always work when you're married.

It might have been a nonissue with someone else. But he married Jada—and she's not okay with it.

"It's always a choice," I turned to Chris. "You're going to disappoint someone: either Jada or Kendra. So, I urge you to pick one, and pick wisely. I know it feels safer to turn and run rather than face another difficult conversation with Jada. But avoiding hard conversations is not the kind of leadership that's going to end this power struggle."

Chris uncrossed his arms and looked at Jada. "I get that. And I'm sorry. I'm sorry that it didn't land well. I'm sorry I wasn't open to hearing what you wanted."

Jada smiled as he said that.

"I don't need the threat of punishment to act. I choose you, and if that means speaking our truth no matter how difficult that may be, I'll do it. You matter more to me than anyone else." Chris squeezed her hand.

"That's all I ask. I don't expect you to have all the answers," Jada said, softening her tone. "Sometimes, I just want you to take me by the hand and say, 'Babe, I got this.'"

"Can you say that again, and drop that toxic little word?"

Chris leaned in before she could rephrase her request and said, "Babe, I got *you*."

"Hold on a second, do you see what happened here?" I wasn't letting go of this moment without calling attention to it.

"What I saw was a physical reconnection and an immediate lowering of the temperature," I smiled. "That was a live-action performance of the 'Pause, Reconnect, Repair' I've been teaching you guys. What do you make of that?"

Jada looked at Chris and smiled. Her shoulders relaxed and, still holding his hand, said, "It feels good. Great actually. I'm really not looking for much. I just want him to be transparent. To tell me what he's going to do."

"Now I know you didn't just say that word again," Chris said with a chuckle.

"Okay—you got me! Old habits die hard," Jada laughed. "I clearly have things to unlearn."

She turned to me.

"I know I can over-focus on every little thing he says or does. But if he can just stop calling our relationship toxic, I'll soften."

Before Chris or I could say anything, Jada caught herself.

"Wait, let me rephrase that," she said. "I want to know from him that hard conversations don't mean our relationship is broken."

"Nicely done!" I praised her.

Chris turned to me. "A lot of this is on me. I turned my back on the little girl inside her when she was upset," he reflected. "I couldn't hear past the yelling or name calling."

"I'm sorry I treated you that way," Jada said as she wiped her eyes. "I've never treated anyone that way. I was scared. And felt like I was crazy."

"I know you're sorry," Chris said, coming to her rescue. "You wanted to feel heard. But I didn't want to listen. I knew you were upset, but I retreated anyway. I'm sorry I made you feel like I was choosing Kendra over you."

This is good. They're finally hearing each other.

"I was afraid she was going to be mad," Chris turned to me and said. "I pushed her away. Instead of going down with the ship, I jumped off before the last passenger got off safely. I didn't lead. I ran."

"That's not an easy thing," I began. "You've been struggling with childhood wounds for a long time. Let's move on to something that does feel good: the final step in the Pause-Reconnect-Repair cycle. What do you think?"

"I'd love that," Chris said with enthusiasm.

"Repair is the last act; it's the owning and forgiving part. But don't go thinking that's one-way. It's both of you accepting the pain and forgiving the hurt."

"So, we're both making an effort to meet in the middle?" Jada asked.

"Exactly. Only, instead of waiting for the other to act, you can move," I said, leaning in. "Take the Kendra situation; Chris needs to set a boundary with that woman—we get it. That's partially why we're here."

"But while the two of you are working yourselves up, no one is looking for the fight-ending phrase couples struggle most to say: 'I'm sorry for how I hurt you.'"

They looked at one another, guilt on their faces.

"Chris, the way you admitted you were wrong showed ownership." I went on. "And Jada, how you acknowledged fighting unfairly showed the same."

"Remember how you did that. Because when you're hurt, your natural inclination is going to be the opposite—to hurt them back. And if both of you start asking 'Who hurts the most?' you'll find yourselves locked in a power struggle you can't win."

"Can't win? But if he's texting Kendra, shouldn't I feel hurt?" Jada asked.

"Of course. But are you sure you're not unintentionally hurting him?" I replied.

"Hurting him? How's that happening here?"

"Look, Chris needs to send out the 'I'm taken' signals. He needs to build a bubble around your relationship. But he also deserves to know that you see when he does. And that you acknowledge how hard it can be for him to stay in the conversation with you when things get loud and personal."

Mouth half open, Jada hadn't taken her eyes off me.

"Two things need to happen in moments of deep emotional pain. One of them you're going to appreciate me saying. The other, you're going to push back on."

"Now I'm really intrigued," Chris said.

"Repair is a selfless act. It requires giving up the moral high ground you think you occupy so you can make space for kindness, grace, and forgiveness."

"I like that. We could use more of that," Chris added. "A lot more."

"After you've paused and physically reconnected long enough that your nervous systems have regulated themselves again, you're going to apologize to one another with the words we all know so well but struggle to say: 'I'm sorry.'"

"No one likes saying that," Chris said.

"Agreed," I replied. "Which is why you're going to practice saying it. And you're not going to add a 'but' to the end of it. That would negate the apology entirely. If you want the word-for-word script, it goes like this: 'I'm sorry for how I hurt you—intentionally and unintentionally.'"

"That last part is the most important. I add that because none of us can truly know all the ways we hurt our spouse. If you did, then repair would be easier because you'd understand their pain."

"Your mission, should you choose to accept it, is to seek forgiveness for the ways that you didn't realize you hurt the other. Hard, I know. But this is essential!"

"That sounds terrible," Jada admitted.

"I know it does. That's why I said you'd hate doing it," I replied with conviction. "But for the sake of making your partner feel safe, could you apologize for ways you've hurt them, even if you can't see those ways?"

"I want to believe I could do that," she answered. "But it seems so hard."

"It doesn't have to be hard, if you both agree on it right here and now," I replied.

"Look, every argument you've had up to this point has been repaired, or you wouldn't be holding hands right now. It just took a lot longer than you'd hoped," I continued. "But imagine with every sincere apology you're met with, 'I appreciate that. It's okay. It's no big deal. I forgive you.' Wouldn't that feel great?"

"That would feel like a breath of fresh air," Chris smiled at Jada.

"It really would," she smiled back.

"What's part two?" Chris asked.

"Part Two is knowing that your partner believes you when you say sorry. If they don't, keep saying it until they do."

"You mean, staying engaged until they really hear you?" Chris asked like the student in the front row.

"Exactly. Commit to getting better at apologizing. Ask more questions to show that you're curious. Make eye contact. And speak like your children are listening to you."

Now, because most of us struggle to get in the mindset of repair, I've got some questions for Jada and Chris—questions you and I could in fact be asking on the regular:

1. *"How can I help you trust me?"*
2. *"How can I help you forgive me?"*
3. *"How can I help you believe me?"*

These simple "How can I?" questions send a powerful message to your partner: you want to end the power struggle.

As a therapist, I can't undo my clients' hurts, and neither can their partner.

But what their partner can do is calm down the inflammation. And that's what a sincere apology does—when it comes *after* reconnection. It melts the anger, tension, and frustration that fan the flames of hurt and replaces them with connection.

Apologizing and forgiving takes practice. And discipline. But as you get better at it, the duration of your conflict will shrink, as it always does. And so will its severity.

I am eager to tell Jada and Chris more.

"The script of that final repair step looks something like this:

'Babe, I'm sorry for what I did and said. I'm sorry I hurt you in ways that I couldn't know or understand.'

'Thank you. I forgive you. I needed to hear that. I'm not happy with what you said, but I know you didn't mean to hurt me.'"

"Does this sound like something you guys can practice? And if either of you want to throw in, 'I love you and I'm not going anywhere,' or 'I don't hate you,' that'd be terrific."

"One hundred percent," Chris nearly shouted.

"Perfect. That makes me really excited for you guys."

"Can I ask one more thing before we leave today?" Jada practically whispered.

"Of course!"

"I'm scared when these sessions end that we're going to backtrack. What do we do then? Is our relationship always going to be hard?"

"I'm going to stop you right there. Those are fear-based questions. I want you to decide right now that your relationship has no space for fear. Unless you allow it. Reject your fear—remember?"

Chris placed his second hand on Jada's.

"History doesn't have to repeat itself. But it will, if you let fear steer the ship. Since the plate incident, have there been any other incidents like that?"

"Not a single one!" Chris said proudly. "Jada didn't mean to go there, and I have zero doubt in my mind that something like that will never happen again."

"So, you see, you are making history. Good history. The kind you want to repeat," I reassured them. "And if this slips next week, if the cycle spins out of control, you have options. What will you do at the first sign of conflict?" I was looking for confirmation that they were equipped with the skills I'd taught them.

Chris went first: "I'm calling timeout, grabbing her hand, and saying, 'Babe, we got this. There's nothing to run from. I'm here with you.'"

"And I'm dropping the 'just' and asking for reassurance," Jada added. "I'll ask, 'Can you help me out here? Can you help me get what I want?'"

"There you go! You don't need fear; you need access to what you've learned here."

Most couples are so afraid of conflict that they don't plan for it. But they should. They should have a plan that helps them move through it—and with a shared identity to support it.

"So, if you trade your old identity, the high-conflict one, what new identity can you guys adopt for your relationship?" I asked.

"Problem-solvers?" Chris asked timidly.

"Exactly," I happily replied.

"You can do better than that," Jada laughed. "We're rockstars!"

"I love it. And if you want to keep that energy going, try asking questions like these from time to time:

What were our successes this week?

When did we feel connected?

What did we do so well that made the repair happen?

How could we get even better at repair?"

I set my notepad down on the coffee table. I wanted them to know I was done taking notes.

"Before you leave, do me a favor: remember that every couple has a painful past. But if you let fear take over, it'll be hard to resist the pull to repeat it," I said. "And instead of worrying about falling back into old habits, focus on falling forward into new ones. You're building a new relationship—so pay attention to that."

They both perked up.

"Think of all the love and safety you've given your kids. And each other over the last couple months. This relationship is beautiful. Does it have a little patina on it? Sure—all relationships do. And that's what makes this one special."

Chris pulled out his phone.

"I'm messaging Kendra as soon as we leave this office," he declared.

Jada looked straight at him and said, "You have no idea how much I love you right now."

Jada and Chris walked out of my office holding hands, as two people who had something to believe in: their relationship.

Chris paused in the hallway to text Kendra.

Jada didn't smother him. She just watched in silence.

They came in thinking their relationship was broken. They were both disappointed in each other and running from fears they couldn't outrun.

But they left a different couple: one with a plan, a new set of skills, and determined to pause when panic strikes, reconnect before resentment sets in, and repair before fear takes over.

Were they fully healed? Not by a long shot.

But did they have the confidence and skills to believe in their marriage again? To trade pain for courage, and fear for forgiveness?

Yes. That's what the hug Chris gave Jada after he sent that text to Kendra told me.

It told me action is what builds a marriage that makes you feel chosen and cherished.

Let's Pause One Last Time...

...before we meet Debbie and Mike.

Most couples think getting rid of what they don't want is more important than getting what they do want.

It's not.

Jada and Chris came in thinking less conflict was the answer to their prayers. In reality, she wanted reassurance that Chris isn't leaving. And he wanted to know he's loved for who he is.

Most couples miss the same thing that Jada and Chris did because they've forgotten the right questions to ask:

"What do you want?"

"And how can I help you get it?"

And if you're a hopeless perfectionist like myself, who squeezes every last drop out of the lemon, here are a few more questions to keep your positive momentum going:

"What were our successes this week?"

"When did we feel connected?"

"What did we do so well that made the repair happen?"

"How could we get even better at repair?"

So decide: Do you want to win at marriage? Or lose?

The couples who win are the ones who move quickly. They don't wait for repair to come to them. They simply go first.

My wife and I can't escape the same standard. When conflict erupts, it's still up to one of us to say:

"I'm sorry for how I hurt you... in ways I know, and in ways I don't."

Want your partner to feel safe? Then ask for what you want. Help them get what they want. And when you mess it up, go first.

That's how you forge a good marriage.

Not with perfection. But with consistency.

Part III

Debbie and Mike: Healing Emotional Decay

Chapter 11

Safety Is a Choice (Predictability Makes Repair Possible)

Sex hurt Debbie. But that wasn't the only reason she stopped.

For years she pushed through the pain. Two years ago, she decided it was too much.

Her doctor said it was endometriosis caused by menopause. But deep down, she knew it was more than hormones. It was Mike's anger.

You'd think the lack of intimacy would've tipped Mike off. It didn't. It was only when Debbie dropped the word *separation* on him that he began to panic.

That's when he picked up the phone and called me.

Mike had met Debbie when she was fresh out of nursing school. He'd just gotten a job at the local telecom. They married a year later and spent

26 years building a good life together. They had one son, Justin; two Harleys that they enjoyed riding on the weekends; and a brown chocolate lab named Digby.

From the outside, things looked good.

Mike worked his way up to supervisor, which allowed Debbie to stay home with Justin. After Justin left for college, the house got really quiet. So Debbie decided to go back to work. She spent a year refreshing her license, and she'd only been back at work for two months when she met Adam.

That's when the cracks in their marriage started to show.

Adam was a nurse, too. He worked on a different floor but filled in on hers when someone got sick. Their "friendship" began on those long shifts together.

When Mike discovered their relationship, he knew it wasn't innocent. That's when he sought help.

After talking nonstop for 20 minutes, he finally let me speak.

"Meet me next Tuesday at 4 p.m.," I told him. "And one more thing. Whatever you do, make sure Debbie joins us."

I wanted to scold him for not waking up sooner, but I had to remain professional.

After a lukewarm introduction and some warm-up chit-chat, it didn't take me long to realize that Debbie wanted this to be a Fix-Mike-And-We're-All-Good dog and pony show. In her mind, this had everything to do with Mike and nothing to do with her.

But that's not how this works, no matter what kind of partner Mike has been.

Yes, she was hurt. I understood that. But for this to work, I needed both of them to participate. And by that, I mean be open to self-reflection.

Debbie didn't know it yet, but I was gearing up to drop that hot potato in her lap—whether she liked it or not.

"Debbie, is there anything you're sorry about?" I couldn't resist asking.

"No. Not really. Can't think of anything, actually," she replied stone-faced.

I was about to ask if she felt her relationship with Adam at work was inappropriate when I caught a flash of guilt in her eye. It was gone in a second. Mike didn't see it. But I did.

Debbie was a caring woman, even if she tried to hide it. The way she looked at Mike told me all I needed to know. She hated how cold she'd become. It was obvious she still loved him, likely more than she was willing to admit to herself—and us.

"Not to put words in your mouth," I said, "but I'm getting the impression we're not here because of Adam. We're here because of how you feel Mike shows up in your marriage. Is that about right?"

"Yes, that's exactly right," she answered.

"And you doubt he's capable of any kind of change?"

"Right again."

I hated being right.

When you meet a couple for the first time, it's tempting to only pay attention to their faces.

Facial expressions tell you what a person's feeling at that exact moment, but they don't tell the whole story.

The body though? The body doesn't lie. It can't.

To sit close to someone means you have to trust them. That's why I take in their body language.

So I smile, nod, and pretend to be the village idiot.

I'm not just listening to their stories in those early minutes. I'm waiting to see what they show me once they've let their guards down.

I'm not just measuring the distance between them; that matters, but not a ton. I'm looking at angles. Two angles, actually.

Do their shoulders form a V or an A? Do their heads lean toward each other or away?

Debbie and Mike? They were sitting like two people who didn't like or trust each other.

Here were two people, married 26 years—with no sex in more than two. And she's not ready to admit to an emotional affair she calls a simple friendship.

I had my work cut out for me.

"I'm going to be very point blank with you," I said, deciding to switch gears. "I can see by the way you're sitting that connection stepped outside for a smoke break in this marriage. But has it always been this frosty between you two? I mean, were there any good times you can recall?"

"Lots!" Mike piped up. "We used to have a ton of fun together. Weekends riding the bikes. Lots of barbecues and softball games."

"Sounds like fun," I said.

"It wasn't all Truman Show, Jonathan," Debbie said, throwing water on our fire. "A lot of those events ended with Mike getting drunk and turning into a Grade-A asshole."

Ooh, I thought, understanding instantly why she wasn't interested in keeping the flame lit.

"Mike's memory only stores the peaches and cream," she continued. "He conveniently forgets what he's like when he's mad. And it's exhausting. You never know what you're going to get: anger or silence."

Debbie shared that they did have some good days—or flat days, as she liked to call them. But they were fewer and farther between. As the years wore on, Mike's anger bled into their relationship, and she started losing hope that Mike was the man she'd grow old with.

"How was I supposed to feel safe?" she asked, rhetorically. "He treated me like crap. Especially on Mondays when he'd sober up."

Mike just sat in silence with his head hung low.

"And don't tell me corking the bottle cured you of anything," Debbie was crying. "Did it ever occur to you that the silent treatment does nothing to hide anger?"

Debbie reached into her purse, pulled out some Kleenex, and wiped her eyes.

"She calls me a dry drunk," he laughed nervously.

But there was nothing humorous about that.

I was genuinely happy for Mike that he was sober, but that doesn't give him license to not talk to his wife for days on end.

That kind of behavior is really damaging. But I hold off on going there yet. There was more to the story I needed to hear.

"Can I say something?" Mike asked meekly.

"Of course. I think now would be a good time."

He looked at Debbie. "I know I was harsh at times. I was angry and impatient. And made you feel stupid for not agreeing with me—"

"Made me feel stupid?" she interrupted him. "Mike, if you didn't like what you were hearing, you'd storm out of the room and slam the door behind you! So no, seeing your smile disappear was the least of my fears. Having to talk to a pouting child about anything real was what drained me."

Mike appeared to have lost the words he was about to share, so Debbie turned to me.

"I know he's already told you we're not intimate anymore. But if he wasn't clear on why, I'll tell you. I don't feel comfortable enough letting him hug me, let alone sleep with me."

That's not good.

Painful intercourse is one thing. But a nervous system so on edge that your wife doesn't want you to touch her, that's something else entirely.

You don't have to be a sex therapist to know this: if a woman doesn't feel safe with you, she's not going to desire you.

That brings me back to that loaded word: *safe.*

No sex in two years? Unsafe. Pain for her when you try? Unsafe. Zero openness in her body when you're sitting beside her? Unsafe.

Those clues tell you everything you need to know. How a man shows up in a woman's life is either going to pull her in or push her away.

I was sitting across from a woman who didn't feel emotionally safe in her husband's presence.

To be fair to Mike, he did quit drinking. That's huge. He's also the one that brought the three of us together. That takes courage—a lot, in fact. At the very least, I knew he wasn't totally oblivious to the seriousness of the situation. There was a good man inside of him, and I was going to find it.

"She makes me sound terrible," Mike found his voice again. "And I probably deserve it."

Nice one, Mike, I let him know with a nod. I was about to praise him for his courage to accept feedback but didn't want to hijack the moment.

"But I never lied to you. Or laid a hand on you," he was looking at Debbie. "I hurt you, yes. But I have always loved you. Broke my back for you. For our son. For our family. I just want the chance to make you feel safe again."

Mike may be out of chances. That'll be up to Debbie to decide.

But in that moment, I saw a man of few words fighting tooth and nail to save his relationship. That's all I needed to know to join him on his mission. But only if he truly commits to making Debbie feel safe.

"Help me understand more of what happens when things turn ugly," I took over the session.

I needed more of the story if I was going to have any hope in making them leave the session feeling better than when they walked in.

"We usually just retreat. We don't sleep in the same room anymore, so going to separate corners has gotten easier over the years," Debbie offered.

"And repair? What's that look like? And how long does it take?"

"Mostly superficial," Debbie said. "Days will pass with little more spoken than a 'Can you pick up Justin after football practice?' Then Mike will eventually come downstairs one morning and act like nothing happened."

"Really, Mike?" I asked. "That doesn't sound very safe to me. Talk to me about what's going on for you."

"I just figured she doesn't want to hear anything I have to say," he said, trying to explain himself.

"Don't turn this around on her," I rebuked him. "You can't let time pass and expect things to go back to normal. That never works the way you want it to. It just makes her walk on eggshells."

Mike hadn't learned that not speaking to his wife for days after a fight wasn't the best plan for repair. All he was doing was breeding resentment over time.

At 51, Debbie was growing tired of how Mike treated her. She didn't want to manage his moods. She wanted to enjoy life as an empty-nester. She had independence. Her own money.

"I don't know if I have it in me to fix this," Debbie said, shaking her head.

There it was, the commitment ambivalence I was worried about. When it shows up, I know I've got about a 1 in 10 chance of saving the marriage. I hoped this was more resignation than a decision Debbie had made for herself.

I let the dust settle on that one and looked at Mike. His heart had sunk.

With his relationship hanging by a thread, he turned to me, "She's talking about moving out and selling the house...going our separate ways."

"I'm sorry to hear that," I said.

My mind had been racing for 45 minutes. I'd seen a lot of damage. This was not going to be easy to triage.

Debbie is exhausted and her nervous system's dysregulated. Mike is working hard to maintain sobriety but needs serious help managing his anger.

They haven't had sex in a long time, and Debbie is getting too emotionally close to a coworker.

Could it get any more complicated for me?

I'm sure it could.

But the problems you know are better than the ones you don't. And if Debbie and Mike have put everything on the table, then I can work with this.

"She's here with us right now, Mike," I said, pulling myself back into our session.

"She's here—just not *with* me," Mike mumbled.

I can see that, Mike. Do I need to point out the angle at which she's sitting to you? I didn't say that, of course.

"How can I be? He either gets angry or goes silent," she said, sighing.

Debbie looked worn out. Time to wind down, I thought.

Only I didn't want to do that on a low note.

It bothers me—a lot—when couples let things go this far.

Everyone's instinct is to find out why. Indifference? Contempt? Mismatched personalities?

But none of that matters right now. And identifying the villain won't help.

You won't find me in a room full of experts discussing what caused Debbie and Mike's marriage to break down. I'll be too busy giving them the question that really matters:

How am I showing up in my partner's life today?

That brings me to the most important task at hand: I've got to help a man win back his wife by showing him how he's been throwing her nervous system out of whack.

He needs to know that his mood and behavior can either sweeten their marriage or poison it.

It's his choice.

Debbie is nowhere close to being sold on the idea of forgiving Mike. And that's completely understandable; he's done a lot of damage.

Even if Debbie were open to the idea right now, Mike is not ready for it. He's in such a state of fight-or-flight that he'll say yes to anything.

But will he actually learn how to regulate his emotions? Or will he just perform for Debbie to keep from losing his marriage?

My goal right now is to get Debbie to lean back into the marriage. But first, she has to hit pause.

I've also got to slow Mike down a little. If I don't, he'll suppress what he wants to see change.

Debbie won't have much bandwidth to hear it, let alone take ownership for the hurts she's caused. But if she can't see the food stuck in her teeth, his rubber band will snap back, and we'll be back here in a year doing this all over again.

I was looking to end the session when Mike dropped even more bad news.

"Her sister has been telling her to leave."

I looked at Debbie. "Is that true?"

"Yes," she answered but softer than I expected. "She knows how bad things have been. And while she loves Mike like a brother, she doesn't like how he treats me."

Well, that's not all bad news, I thought.

"She knows about Adam, too," Mike added. "I'd love to know if she approves of that."

"She's not telling me to leave you for him, if that's what you're thinking!"

"Well, what is she thinking then?"

"I don't know… that someone is out there who could treat me better than you perhaps."

"Sounds to me like he's an excuse to leave!"

"I don't need an excuse to leave, Mike!" Debbie fired back. "If I needed to look for anything, it'd be to find the self-hate to stay."

This session was going from low to lower, really fast. I needed to step in.

"I need you guys to stop talking before this gets any more out of hand," I ordered them. "Can you do that?"

I took their silence as consent.

"Great," I said, lowering my voice.

"Mike, hear me when I say this: Debbie's relationship with Adam is a symptom. People don't catch feelings for another person like they do a cold. They do it because their relationship is suffering from serious emotional decay, and they look for connection elsewhere. It's not okay, but that's usually how it goes."

Mike nodded like the message was sinking in.

"Debbie, you deserve to be with someone who makes you feel good."

She nodded.

"I want to feel safe. But my walls are up. Anger stole my husband—and now I'm left grieving the thought of not celebrating our 50th wedding anniversary."

"50th what?" I asked Debbie, "I missed that. Can you repeat what you said?"

"I said that I was sad about the thought of not celebrating our 50th," she replied.

And there it was. Debbie had just opened the door I'd spent the last hour looking for. I'd been dodging their pain all session, and now I had a chance to end it on a high note. And get that pause on separation I'd been hoping for.

"If you can be sad about that, does that mean there could be more here than just pain?" I asked.

"Of course there is," she looked at Mike and gave a hint of a smile for the first time all session. "He does a lot for us. He takes care of the house, and Digby, our dog. He's always there for Justin."

"Okay, look. I don't want to force you guys into anything. If I tried, it wouldn't work anyway," I began. "But can we zoom out and see if there is more to this marriage than just what hurts? And I'm not talking about home maintenance. I mean the stuff that matters more than that."

"What does that look like?" Mike said, jumping up for the treat like a golden retriever.

"Let's book our next session and I'll tell you all about it."

I crossed my fingers that Debbie would show up.

Let's Pause Here...

People say you need emotional connection before you can have intimacy.

Let me translate that into a language people actually understand...

Something less vague. Something you can actually use.

You need to freaking like the person you're with.

Is it any surprise that your presence has the power to make your spouse smile or wince?

It shouldn't.

People want to feel emotionally safe inside of their relationship.

And when they feel safe, they like being around each other.

Which is why it shouldn't be surprising that the kind of safety people crave is the predictable kind. If your partner doesn't know who's walking through the door at 5 o'clock, they'll never relax.

I've known women so exhausted from wondering which version of their husband would walk through the door that they secretly wished no one would.

And I've known men who sat in their driveway for 15 minutes trying to work up the courage to go inside because they didn't know who was waiting for them when they did.

That's why this isn't a men's issue or a women's issue.

It's an us issue.

It took me 12 years to understand that the best way to put a smile on Meredith's face was by asking: which version of me was she getting today?

That question changed the course of our relationship.

And so if you want your spouse to smile at you again, like mine did, then start by asking yourself:

"How am I showing up in their life today?"

Then change one thing right now.

I need to prep you, though.

You're going to want to be genuinely curious when you ask, and brutally honest when you answer. Otherwise, the relationship you truly want will remain a thought experiment.

As harsh as it sounds…

If you're unwilling to look at what you bring into your partner's life, don't be surprised if they stop wanting you in it.

Chapter 12

Consistency Is the Antidote to Despair (Don't Wait for Safety to Grow)

"We had a giant fight on the weekend," Debbie kicked us off at the start of our second session.

I guess we're not circling back to the joy we'd talked about last session.

"I went riding. Alone again," Mike added.

Debbie rolled her eyes when he said that.

"Can we just tell him the elephant in the room?" Mike snapped as he shot Debbie a side-eye.

Ahhh, I should have known…couples never put it all on the table in the first session.

"My father's got cancer. Colorectal cancer," she told me.

"You're leaving something out," Mike said pointedly.

"I'm getting to it!" Debbie was clearly annoyed. "Anyway. I had to take him in for chemo last week. On Wednesday. Mike's birthday."

"Okay…that's unfortunate timing…but what else am I missing?" I asked.

"Uh, the fact that Debbie chose him again." Mike was clearly upset.

The pain in that was hard to miss.

"I'm sorry to hear that," I offered him.

"I'm sorry, too. Sorry I had to ride alone. Again," Mike said as he crossed his arms.

I looked at Debbie. Nothing. She just stared straight ahead.

"All her dad has to do is pick up his phone and she comes running," Mike added.

"He needed to go, Mike! What was I supposed to do?"

Debbie turned to me.

"We have a volunteer who usually takes him, but he had trouble with his car," she said.

Mike looked at me.

"Whatever," he said. "He's a selfish asshole."

The look on Debbie's face told me she'd heard that before.

I could already see where this was going.

They've been married nearly three decades—and they're still arguing about her father. The emotional tsunami is coming.

Mike clearly doesn't have a lot of love for his father-in-law.

Debbie was about to tell me why.

"Mike has always accused my dad of not liking him," Debbie said as she broke her stare.

"I think you're missing a rather key detail in there, sweetheart," Mike said sharply.

"What, that he's abrasive? Get over it, Mike. You're a grown man," she said, angrily. "Why do you care about what he thinks of you anyway?"

"Well, probably because you act like his opinion matters more than mine," Mike shot back.

He turned to me.

"I've been nothing but nice to the man," he said. "Always been respectful—even though he's never earned it."

"If exploding with anger every time his name comes up counts as respectful, then yeah, you've done a great job," Debbie added.

"How many baseball games have I sat through because he 'had' to watch his favorite team?" Mike exploded. "How many times do I need to walk through his front door without receiving so much as a handshake?"

"Catch your breath, Mike," I ordered him.

"Thank you," Debbie said. Her look told me she needed a witness to that.

"This goes back to the beginning. When Mike asked my dad if he could marry me...," she started to say.

"Yeah," Mike said, interrupting. "You remember what he said?"

"How could I forget?" Debbie answered him. "I've heard it a hundred times."

Mike turned to me.

"I drove to his house and asked for her hand; he's a traditional guy, and I thought it would be a gesture he'd appreciate. His response? 'You seem like a nice guy, and I'm glad Debbie's happy. You didn't go to college, but I guess I won't hold that over you.' Can you imagine saying that to your future son-in-law?"

I looked at Mike. His shoulders were hunched over. He looked sad.

"I'm guessing there was no handshake. No 'welcome to the family,'" I made the mistake of asking.

"Nailed it!" Mike answered.

That must have hurt. It probably hurt a lot as a young man to be treated like that.

I'm the father of two girls and look forward to the day when I can welcome two sons into our family. Unfortunately, Mike was not so lucky.

"This is starting to make sense to me," I said, softly. I wanted to turn the temperature down and it's important to see if Mike will follow my lead.

"You've felt like this for a long time," I said to him. "On the outside, that is."

"Not making me feel included, I can get over that," he replied. "But the fact that she never says anything to him about it...well, that hurts."

And there it was. The painful emotional truth Mike has struggled with all these years.

He looked at Debbie. "He's always your first thought. 'My dad wants this...my dad needs that.' What about me? I needed a wife who didn't make me feel like I was getting the scraps of her attention after she'd given most of it to him."

"My dad's sick, Mike," she said.

Then she turned to me.

"My mother died when I was five years old. My father never remarried. He's got no one to help him. What was I supposed to do, not take him for his appointment?"

I felt sorry for Debbie. She's being pulled in two directions. And she doesn't see how painful it is for Mike.

"You know, I don't even mind that she had to cancel plans on my birthday. It's that she doesn't feel bad about it. That's what hurts."

Ooh, that stung. It was time to jump in before things got hot again.

"Let me get this straight," I said. "Debbie, you see your role as taking care of two people."

"Three actually," she corrected me. "If you include our son, Justin."

I turned to Mike.

"And you'd say she's not there for you at all, correct?"

"That's right. In 26 years she's never had my back," he answered.

"I understand that, Mike. We don't need to go back there. This is hard enough without the fine details," I said, firmly.

Back to Debbie.

"So, you're choosing to take care of your dad right now," I said. "The one who needs you most?"

"Jonathan, I'm not trying to be difficult here," Mike interrupted, again. "But that hasn't changed in 26 years."

"I understand and appreciate you saying it that way, Mike."

I paused to let his comment clear out of the room.

"But she's not choosing her dad over you—even if it feels like it," I said. "She is a nurse, after all. Taking care of people is what she does well."

I looked at Debbie.

"The problem is, marriages don't survive on leftovers," I said to her. "And right now, Mike doesn't feel chosen."

Debbie took a second to respond.

"I never thought about it like that," she said.

It's going to be hard to get Debbie and Mike on the same page when it comes to her dad.

"There should be two people in a marriage. Not three," he said to me.

Four actually, if you include Adam, I nearly said under my breath.

"I can't argue with you there, Mike."

"But that's not what we have here," he continued. "I've competed with him for her time since the day we married. And now that he's old and sick, I stand even less of a chance."

I have no choice but to believe what Mike is saying. It's reality—his reality. And it needs to be honored.

Debbie's loyalty to her father stretched way back—to early days when it was just the two of them navigating life without a mother or a wife.

Mike understands their relationship. But it frustrates him. And that it comes out as anger doesn't help his case.

She feels attacked, and loses curiosity and empathy along with it. That only makes Mike attack again.

The fight over Mike's canceled birthday was only the latest round in a decades-long struggle, a struggle that got worse two years ago when Debbie's father got sick.

Mike wants his wife. Debbie wants a husband who makes her feel safe. And I want them riding Harleys together again.

Those goals are going to be hard to achieve if Debbie and Mike can't agree on what the role of a daughter is.

In Mike's eyes, that role shouldn't stop Debbie from putting him first.

I wasn't about to remind him that doctors don't treat a broken leg just because it arrives in the ER before the heart patient—but I didn't want to get sidetracked.

"When we were younger, I was working a lot," Mike said, softening up, "I didn't have time to give a damn about her father. I was drinking then, too. And that helped, a lot."

"Makes sense," I said, nodding slightly.

"But I'm sober now. And Justin's gone. I don't want to have to compete for my wife's attention. And when I tell her that, she gets defensive," Mike said softly.

"That's because of your tone; it's scary," Debbie responded.

"Scary tone, happy tone, no tone," he said, rolling his eyes now. "Doesn't matter how I say it. I'm still coming in second."

When Mike said that, my stomach sank. He's just as exhausted as she is in this marriage.

And it made perfect sense. Because on paper, they functioned well together. Their roles were clear: taking care of the house, Justin's football, managing finances, etc. It worked for them, and appreciation was felt by both.

But Mike wanted more than a thank-you. He wanted her time and the message it sent him: that he mattered.

Debbie's father made that hard for her.

After her mother's death, her father leaned on her—hard. And when she grew up, she became the one he called, the one who couldn't say no.

At no point did Debbie stop to ask:

"What does loyalty to my husband actually look like?"

I can't blame her, though. Not a lot of people think about the importance of that kind of loyalty in a marriage. They focus on fidelity and honesty and think that's it. But it's not.

Marriages need two people in them—not three.

"I've never said no to you," Mike said to Debbie. "Never once did I say you couldn't be there for him when he told us about the cancer."

"I know," she said, making eye contact with him.

Good one, Mike.

Despite the rough start, we've made progress.

The pain is coming out in a safe place. If Debbie's talking divorce, it means she wants out of the pain. Better she let it out here than let it out by leaving Mike.

And there's still good here. Mike wants to spend time with his wife. That means he loves her and is motivated to change.

He's also shown he can change. He fought hard for sobriety—and won. That tells me change is more than possible here; it's probable.

In any crisis, you've got two options: divorce or repair.

Both are painful.

Choosing divorce gives people certainty, something we all love.

Choosing repair? Not so much. There are no guarantees of success, and people don't like that.

That's what makes this job so hard.

Since Debbie is leaning out, I need her to see Mike as a good man—a safe man—if there's any hope that repair will work.

So how do you create hope in a marriage that feels hopeless?

First, you stop looking at the pain. Couples in crisis can't build a case for staying if there's no joy worth staying for. So we look for what feels good; the smaller, the better.

Second, you have to take them back. Back to when things felt good. If they can't reconnect with all the reasons why they chose each other in the first place, they'll never connect with the reasons why they should choose each other again.

As it sits, Debbie doesn't like Mike. Or at least parts of him.

That has to change.

But it won't unless Mike treats her differently. And that requires Mike to feel good about himself.

If he doesn't believe he can be seen as a good man again, he won't try. He won't put in the effort to treat her better.

So that's where we have to start: in their past.

There's a treasure trove of good in it. And taking inventory of it is my best shot at getting them to see it.

"Debbie, I was wondering," I said, cautiously. "Last time we met, I asked you to recall any moments when you felt safe in your marriage."

"Yes, I remember."

"Well, I'm not trying to make Mike sound like a saint, but I have to wonder how safe it feels to be married to someone who wants to spend time with you. Seems to me like that would keep you warm at night."

Debbie tucked her hair behind her ear.

"I suppose," she said.

That's it? I was hoping for more. She's going to make me work for this, I thought.

"Have you acknowledged that before?"

"To who? To Mike?"

"How about yourself," I said, reversing her.

"Look, I know what you're doing...."

Uh-oh. Too fast, I thought. The shift in tone felt like I'd just stepped outside and had a blast of winter air shoot down my back.

"I'm not sure I can blow smoke up Mike's ass right now," she said.

"I totally get that," I replied meekly. But I'm not letting this go.

"He just said he's not trying to talk me up," Mike said, coming to my defense.

"I appreciate that, Mike. But I can handle this," I said, waving him off. "Look, I'm not asking you to do anything you're not ready for. But what if you gave yourself permission to see what's good here without the pressure of stepping back in?"

I had to be careful. I didn't want to push too hard.

"Whether you're looking for an exit or not, nothing needs to be decided just because you've started down one path or another," I said. "There's something to learn here—if you're willing to have the conversation."

"I can see that," she agreed.

I breathed a little easier.

"I'd like to see the good things here. But...," she trailed off.

I didn't say anything. You can't work harder than your clients, as my supervisor Susan likes to say.

"I'm sorry, it just feels safer not opening the door for him," she finally said.

"There's nothing to apologize for," I said, reassuring her. "You have good reason to want to feel safe. But since we're on the topic, can I get your opinion on that?"

"Yeah, sure."

"When Justin was growing up, would you have given me 10 minutes with him to talk about what he was planning to do after high school?"

"I'm sorry?" Debbie looked perplexed.

I love when my clients can't figure out where I'm going. It makes my point land harder when they do.

"I was about to say that I'd have loved to tell him not to go to college."

By the look on Mike's face, I'd completely lost him, too.

"Would you have been okay with that? With me telling him college was a bad idea because he didn't know what to study? And that good schools are hard to get into, so why bother even applying?"

"No, that wouldn't be okay," Mike answered for them both.

"But that would be safer for him, no?" I pushed back. "I'd be protecting him from disappointment…keeping him 'safe.'"

"Well, uh…," Mike started to say something. But I cut him off.

"Not knowing how to do something—or if you'll succeed if you try—isn't the problem. It's believing you're unsafe because of it."

I let that sink in.

"People are afraid of what they don't know. They're especially afraid of their partner changing. That's what makes marriage feel unsafe—because it's always changing."

"How so?" asked Debbie.

"Because people do change. So by that logic, marriage would forever feel unsafe."

I turned to Mike.

"What really makes people feel safe in a marriage is how we treat them," I said.

I wanted to signal to Mike that letting his anger dictate how he treats Debbie is a sure-fire way to push her away.

"Has your marriage changed?" Debbie asked.

"So much you'd want a seatbelt just to watch it from the stands," I said.

I let that reassure her.

"Look, you can leave," I said. "Sell your house, the Harleys, and everything else. You know, walk away because it feels unsafe trying something different.

Or, you can accept that this process feels uncertain. And tell yourself that just because it feels unsafe, you're not going to stop trying."

I let that land.

"Change is coming. It may be the end of your marriage. Or the birth of a new one. But you won't know which, until you try."

I looked at Debbie, then Mike.

"If you're only willing to see the pain here, then I've a good idea how this ends," I said. "But I don't think you want that."

"I see your point. And I'll play along. But I am giving *you* a short leash," Debbie said with a little smile.

"It's really not me you're giving the leash to," I said.

I looked at Mike to make sure she knew who I was talking about.

"I've got a ton of faults. And I don't know all the ways I hurt you," Mike said, like an actor who knew his lines. "I don't know how to get you to forgive me. But I don't want to give up on us."

"I like how you said that, Mike," I said, acknowledging his entrance back into the conversation.

"Do you think you're ready to look for more than pain here in this relationship?" I asked Debbie.

"Yes, I think I can," she replied.

"Good," I said, and then turned to Mike, nodding at him. "I know you're up for it. But you gotta promise me one thing."

"Of course, what is it?"

"There won't be any swapping out pain for joy here if you don't promise Debbie the safety she deserves. That means kicking anger out of your relationship like the houseguest that's overstayed his welcome. So I'm going to share an important concept with you."

It was clear that Mike needed help controlling his anger. So I took a few minutes to teach him about a concept that my therapist, Jim, had introduced me to: the idea of paper tigers and how they're different from real tigers.

Because of the trauma I experienced as a child, my brain was wired to send floods of cortisol through my body—enough to trigger a full fight-or-flight response, no matter how serious the issue actually was.

As a result, I interpreted every frustration, moment of stress, or annoyance the same way: as a real tiger. Serious threats coming to hurt me.

Jim helped me reframe these moments as "paper tigers." They were situations that were never as big a deal as my brain was making them out to be.

Ever since that lightbulb went off in my head, I've been able to say to myself, "Jonathan, chill out. It's just a paper tiger. Not something worth destroying your relationship over."

Sometimes Meredith would be able to say the same thing to me. Sometimes not.

But when I remembered to see things that way, it helped me come back down to Earth—quickly.

When I shared this concept with Mike, he got it immediately. It made sense to him and to Debbie.

And it gave him something more than just hope.

It gave him a simple tool to help fix his tone and regulate how he showed up for Debbie.

And if he used it consistently, he'd have a fighting chance of getting her to come back again next week.

"I want to do that, a thousand percent!" Mike said. "I'm just scared that I won't be able to."

"Well, that sounds to me like you guys have one more thing in common," I smiled. "Fear. But you know what fear hates most around here?"

"What's that?" Mike asked.

"Me," I replied. "Because in this office, no one gets away with having a fixed mindset. If I can change and my wife can change, then you two can change."

I checked the time. Almost there.

"Change is going to happen," I added. "You just have to have the courage to embrace it."

"Makes sense," Mike said with a hopeful smile.

I gathered my notes.

"We've done a lot here today," I said. "How about, as we wrap up, you acknowledge yourselves for showing up and doing the work?"

"Sounds good," they said in unison.

"Next week, Mike, I want to hear about how you single-handedly took down one of those paper tigers we talked about. And Debbie, I promise we'll make it an hour worth your time, or I'll pay you for the session."

"That won't be necessary, Jonathan. I'll be here regardless."

They weren't holding hands when they left my office. But I took it as a win when she let him help her put her jacket on.

Not bad.

But we've still got work to do.

Let's Pause Here...

I'm a yeller. Well, at least I used to be. It's what my father raised me to be good at.

To be honest, it's a really effective strategy for creating distance from the people who hurt you. But it's not so helpful when it comes to building a long, happy marriage.

Whatever behavior you're struggling with, I want you to be honest with yourself:

"Am I pulling them in...or pushing them away?"

Your partner is the one person in the world you're looking to share your life with. But they'll lose the desire to if your unboundaried behavior goes unchecked.

If you're tired of your spouse calling you an asshole, do yourself a favor: believe them.

Then resolve to do something about it.

And while you're at it, do me a favor: don't chase "safety." I know it sounds good. But it's vague, and too abstract.

What your marriage actually needs is consistency.

So instead of asking, "How can I make my relationship feel safe?" start with:

"What's one behavior that's hurting it that I will eliminate—starting today?"

You can't build a safe relationship if your partner doesn't like how you treat them. And that's especially true if your own pain blinds you to the way that you hurt them.

I made a vow to stop yelling at my wife. It took 10 years and a ton of effort to show her that she wasn't married to a tyrant.

Eventually, she started to believe it.

But only because I made it my mission, every single day.

Chapter 13

Act and You'll Receive (Forgiveness Is the Byproduct, Not the Goal)

"So, tell me. What's been better since last week?"

Most couples have no idea how to answer this. They're mentally prepared to be asked what's been worse.

My question's contrarian, but it works. It gets them focused on connection, not conflict. And I knew it was the best way to open our third session.

"Better than last week?" Debbie cracked a smile. "I'll let Mike explain that one."

Did she just let in a little light? That may be a tiny bit of hope making an appearance in my office.

"It wasn't that big of a deal," Mike picked up the ball. "We rode out to visit our son. We like to embarrass him by pulling up on our bikes."

"What a nice way to end the weekend!"

"It actually went really well," he continued. "What she's referring to was me keeping my cool on the drive there."

"Oh. How so?"

"There was roadwork going on, and we were running late. I thought I could take a shortcut, but we ran into construction, and it turned into a longcut."

"That's frustrating," I said, acknowledging the annoyance.

"Yeah, for sure," Mike smiled. "I felt myself getting really pissed off. But all I could do was think of that 'paper tiger' phrase you used. I couldn't get it out of my head."

"Hah!" I said, barely containing my excitement.

"I was just as startled as you are now," Debbie chimed in.

"I'm sure you were. That's a big deal."

"I could actually feel my hands grip the handle bars tighter by the second. But something slowed down inside of me, and I told myself to shrug it off. Better to get there with a smile than a burst blood vessel."

"Fantastic choice," I nodded at Debbie to punctuate the win.

"I agree. It was nice seeing him protect his happy place," she said. "It's the way it should be."

"Sounds to me like that was safety at 30 miles an hour," I looked at her.

"It's definitely a start."

I turned to Mike. "How would it feel to get more consistent at that?"

"That'd be great. You said you'd show me," Mike reminded me.

"Indeed, I did. Let's do that right now. Sound good?" I asked, knowing the answer.

"I'd love to," he replied.

I half expected Mike to pull out a notepad. But he leaned forward instead. I noticed Debbie did, too. Ah, she's curious. Another win. Her chill wasn't as cold.

"Mike, did you know how to ride motorcycles when you bought your Harleys?"

"Haha. That was years ago," he laughed. "And no, I didn't. Not at all in fact. But what's that got to do with anger?"

"I'm really glad you asked that," I replied. "And I'm fully aware that if I can't give you a good reason, you're going to wonder what you're paying me for."

They both laughed. Another win.

"Entertain me, will you? Why motorcycles? What made you want to learn to ride one?"

"We were doing well financially. I'd just got promoted, and Justin was at the age that he could be left on his own. We always talked about getting bikes. And since we both love adventure, we said 'let's do it.' So we bought two and figured we'd learn to ride them or have to sell them."

"So, just to confirm, you bought the bikes, even though you couldn't ride them?" I asked.

"Yes," he answered.

"But why motorcycles? Why go through all the trouble to learn how to ride them when you could just roll the car windows down if you want to feel wind in your air as you cruise the outdoors?"

"It's not the same. It doesn't look the same. Feel the same. Or sound the same."

"But you couldn't have known that when you bought the bikes," I challenged him.

"Oh, I knew," he said. "One day, a guy on our softball team showed up to a game on his Harley. You only had to see the smile on his face to know how much he was loving life."

"And you wanted to feel that, too?" I asked.

"I took one look at Debbie and said, 'I'm buying a bike.' She just said to me, 'I know.' The next Saturday, I walked into the dealership and bought my first bike. Still have it to this day."

"Now we're getting somewhere," I said, feeling the momentum grow.

"And was the handlebar mustache part of that vision?" I asked him.

"Heck, yeah," he laughed.

"So, you had a vision. And a goal. You knew what you wanted and decided to go for it, right?"

"Pretty much," he said. "There's safety you have to know about in order to ride a motorcycle, but I knew I could learn it."

"Music to my ears, Mike." I said, barely containing myself. "You knew what you wanted and decided to go for it."

"That's right," he agreed.

"But you didn't go all in on motorcycles," I continued. "You went all in on yourself. And Debbie."

I let that sink in.

"Mike, I need you to tap into two things right now," I continued. "The two things a man needs when he finds himself in your shoes."

"What's that?"

"Your ability to see yourself as the man you want to be and the courage to become him," I replied.

"Just like motorcycles, if you didn't think you could get sober, you'd never have tried," I continued. "You'd have been afraid to look at yourself in the mirror had you failed."

"I can see that."

"Your wife, sitting beside you, isn't ready to set her purse down on the floor."

Mike looked at Debbie's purse in her lap.

"That should tell you she's not feeling fully relaxed right now."

"I never noticed that," he said, nodding.

"Good thing you've been paying me to notice these things," I quipped back.

You could almost see the lightbulb turn on Mike's head.

"I want you to read the room, Mike. Read Debbie's body language. Tune into her energy. Can you do that?"

"I'd like to try."

"Don't try anything, Mike! Let yourself," I said with more passion than needed. "Allow yourself to tune into her. Allow yourself to go back to those early days and be the man she fell in love with. That man is still inside you. He hasn't gone anywhere. You simply have to let him back out. Let out the man who protected her from the world. Not the man the world needs to protect her from."

Tears begin to fall down his cheek. I started thinking I pushed him too far.

"Are you okay? Is this too much?" I asked, modeling for him the very questions I needed him to get good at asking.

"No…no. I need this," he answered me. "She deserves this."

"She does indeed. She deserves your safety. As you do hers."

"So how do I give it to her?"

"With consistency," I answered him. "Right now, she doesn't know she's married to. She doesn't trust who you are."

I let that sit.

"So you have to change that, Mike," I continued. "And you do that with questions—lots of questions."

A quick glance at the purse on the floor tells me that Debbie let her guard down, just a little.

Good. I just hope Mike doesn't squander his opportunity.

He's going to have to follow through. His tears tell me he's ready. But tears and readiness are meaningless without action.

We're not going to undo three decades of pain in one session. But we do need to mute it for the time being. If not, we're going to fall down a hole so deep, you'd need to send a search party to find us.

The first step of this journey is to get Debbie to lean back in.

And she'll only do that if Mike puts gas in her tank.

That means showing up with a little self-reflection and a side order of courage.

Correction. He'll need a lot of self-reflection.

I'll reassure him that progress doesn't require perfection. It would be ridiculous to think that's even possible.

Mike needs to show Debbie that he's capable of growing.

He saw a sober life on a Harley, and he acted. That vision compelled him to take action. If he did it back then, he can do it again.

Debbie is going to want to see progress if she's to trust Mike again. That means holding space for her when they don't see eye to eye. And making an effort to show he understands her desire to care for her sick dad.

Even though Mike's grown tired of Debbie's caregiver guilt, he has to make a choice: Does he let anger push her away? Or use self-control to pull her in?

He has to make emotional maturity the new theme for their relationship. Not Harleys. Not sobriety. Those are yesterday's.

When Debbie sees change enter the room, her desire to leave him will exit it.

In fact, the more he shows up, the more open she'll be to seeing her mistakes. And when she does, Mike will know that things in their marriage have flipped from crisis to repair mode.

So here's where Mike starts. He has to resist the urge to ask, "Why do you want to leave?"

That question will only connect her to the reasons she wants to leave the marriage. Not helpful.

Mike doesn't need subjective truths right now. He needs direction.

And he gets that by asking her how, when, and what caused their marriage to feel broken.

He needs questions that show he's open to self-reflection. And questions that'll give him something to act on.

Questions like these:

1. *"When did you stop feeling chosen by me?"*
2. *"What pain of yours have I caused?"*
3. *"What trust did I break and never fully repair?"*
4. *"How can I show up better for you? And what does that look like?"*
5. *"If you believed I could fight for us—consistently—what would I be doing?"*

See how I phrased these questions?

They're a combination of *how-can-I-help-you-release-the-hurt* and *what-could-I-have-done-better* questions.

Taken together, the theme of these questions is:

"What do I need to do to slow this ship down, bring it to a stop, and turn it around?"

Debbie isn't going down without a fight, and so "turn this ship around" is not her goal here. It's not even on her radar.

That's Mike's goal.

Mike has broken her trust with his negative behavior, repeatedly throughout their marriage.

She's going to fire back with, "Words mean nothing right now. I need to see action."

Debbie's going to need time to soften.

Trust and safety is what she's craving. And right now, she's finding it—just not with Mike.

Remember Adam at the nurse's station? He's waiting for her with her favorite Starbucks bevvy and an attentive ear. And whether Debbie sees their friendship as a problem is irrelevant.

Sure, she considers them to be just friends. She may not even think she's got feelings for him.

But bless her naive little heart, because you can be almost certain that if things don't turn around with Mike, she risks falling into Adam's arms faster than a house on stilts rolls down a hillside when the mud starts flowing.

But Mike shouldn't despair. I'm not. And neither should you.

Why?

Because it's never too late to turn things around.

Mike asking a few self-reflective questions won't cure all his marital troubles. The questions I gave him are not that effective. But they're not completely ineffective either.

If used correctly, they can open doors. They're invitations, and that's the way he should see them. They're the play to call when starting on the 20-yard line.

"Okay, I like the questions," Mike said deliberately. "But I still have no clue what's going to convince Debbie that our relationship can change."

"That's the best part, Mike!" I declared.

"Okay…"

"You don't have to know how," I continued. "You have to act. Make a decision, set your pride down, and start. Debbie's answers will tell you what play to call next!"

"I think I can do that," he said.

"Great."

I looked at Debbie to see if she was still with us. I wasn't ready to put her on the hot seat, though. I needed Mike to know something first.

"It may seem like I'm making it out to be," I began. "But this isn't all your fault."

"I know. It takes two to tango," he uttered.

"Debbie," I said, finally making eye contact. "Back to the question I've been waiting to ask you: can you give Mike the time to see where this can go?"

"I, uh…," she started to say.

"Sorry," I said, interrupting her. "Don't answer that! I don't want you to—not yet anyway. I'd rather just plant the seed, if that's okay."

"Okay," she murmured.

Mike needs time right now, like a dog needs a bone.

But as their therapist, I can't lose sight of the fact that Debbie has one foot out the door. Mike's leaning in, and hard, because he risks losing everything he's worked for all these years.

He loves Debbie. Deeply.

But right now, she's not interested in hearing how she's contributed to their situation. So I'll still push, just very carefully.

I turned to her.

"When you think about your relationship, what words come to mind?"

It doesn't take her a moment. "Emotionally exhausting."

"That's really hard," I reflected, acknowledging her pain. It's more than a flesh wound, but at least we have all our limbs.

And now I have the exact words Debbie uses to describe her relationship.

Why's that important? Because I need to speak her language.

If I don't, I'll lose her.

Debbie needs to feel heard and understood. That takes time, and the right questions.

Now that I know what she doesn't want—exhaustion—I can get busy finding out what she does. And so can Mike.

Does that mean he can give it to her? Not right away.

He may have shown her a glimpse of the old Mike on the ride last weekend, but we've still got a long way to go.

"I'm sorry things are so exhausting," I said, repeating her words back to her.

I don't want to force her to ignore her pain, so my follow-up is gentle.

"Can I ask, are there any moments in your marriage, like last Sunday, when it doesn't feel unsafe?"

"I really can't think of any," she replied.

Of course you can't, I wanted to say.

But I let her sit in silence instead. I'm not moving away from this. If I do, I dismiss 26 years of Mike's commitment to their marriage.

Mike's made mistakes, but there's a good man inside of him. If I back down and let Debbie walk out of here without acknowledging the good in their marriage, then I've failed. I'll have let Mike down.

"I'm sorry. Not much comes to mind right now," she stressed.

"Take all the time you need, Debbie. I'm not going anywhere. And we know Mike isn't either."

And that is how you gently—but with patience—remind someone that the exit won't be free.

If I let Debbie off the hook without asking her to see the joy in their marriage, I validate the echo chamber of self-affirmation she finds herself in, and I'll squander Mike's chance at repair.

For distressed couples like Debbie and Mike, pain and any talk of it should be avoided at all costs.

There's a time for pain talk, but this isn't it. It needs to be replaced with joy talk. Without finding the joy in their marriage, I'm not sure we'll make it to another session.

After a moment of silence, Debbie finally cracked.

"He always made time for Justin," she blurted out.

"Isn't that to be expected as a dad?" I said, pushing back.

"Well yeah, but he had to work a lot. Many late nights and weekends."

"And that didn't stop him from spending time with him?"

"Never. In fact, he'd often take Friday afternoons off for Justin's away games."

"So that explains their close relationship?"

"Yes, they're two peas in a pod."

"What's that all about? Why was that important to you?" I turned to Mike and asked.

"Because I didn't have a dad. My folks split when I was 13 and bi-weekly visits were too much of a commitment for him."

"So, you wanted something different for Justin?"

"Of course. I wanted him to have a father."

"You wanted to be a nurturer?"

"Seems like a word you'd use to describe a woman, but yes, I suppose so."

"And a provider?" I asked Debbie. "Did he do a good job at that, too?"

"Yes. Always. My card was never declined."

"So as much as he was consistent in his anger, he was consistent as a nurturing father and provider, too, if I have it right."

"You do. And yes, he was…is, I should say."

"And has that ever entered the conversation?" I said, about to tee off.

"In what way?"

"Well, nothing is all good or all bad, especially a marriage," I answered her. "But I have to wonder if his consistency as a father and provider is worth adding to the balance sheet. You know, if we're adding his anger to the balance sheet, shouldn't we include some assets to that statement?"

"We could. Or should, I suppose."

"What do you suppose stopped you from keeping those qualities of Mike top of mind?"

"Her father," Mike interjected.

Umph. We're hitting that wall of hurt again, I thought.

"Leave my dad out of this!" Debbie punched back.

"I would if he actually was," Mike countered.

I needed to intervene. And fast. We've made too much forward progress for me to let this go sideways.

"I can feel your pain, Mike," I said. "But this is a moment when you lean into vulnerability, not anger."

"Okay, I'll try."

"Good," I said, relieved he walked that back.

"Mike, I want you to feel confident when you leave this office," I continued. "Let's bring curiosity back in here. If you want to win her heart and mind, you're going to have to shake things up first."

"Uh, okay. But I'm not trying to scare her or anything."

"That's not what we're doing. But you will if you keep leading with your pain."

I turned to Debbie.

"The time's going to come when you have to see your role here," I said gently. "That's going to be hard, I know. But I know you don't think that Mike's the only one that has a side of the street to sweep."

"Of course not," she conceded.

I put my notebook down and cupped my hands, pretending like I'm holding their relationship in them.

"Imagine I'm holding a snow globe. And inside it are two figurines. A handsome groom and his beautiful bride."

I paused for a moment.

"And when that snow globe is sitting in a display case, the snow settles, and you can see them plain as day."

Mike looked at Debbie and smiled. Good. They were tracking me.

"But when someone comes around and shakes that snow globe up, you can't see them clearly anymore. You have to wait till the snow settles again to do that."

"And that's what happens when Debbie's dad comes along and wrecks my birthday?" Mike asked.

"Exactly. That's exactly what happens when someone shakes our relationship bubble," I replied.

"I can see that," Debbie said, acquiescing.

"I'm not asking you to feel connected when everyone and their brother wants to make it hard for you. The shift to make is protecting your bubble in the first place—like taping a sign to the snow globe that says, 'No touching without asking staff first.'"

Their heads nodded. The plane landed.

"Back to you, Mike," I looked at him. "In the softest, most nonthreatening way, you're going to invite Debbie to see how her decisions are impacting you."

"I follow you," he said. "I can see where you're going here."

"Good," I said. "Now, very simply, ask Debbie, 'What message should I be receiving when your dad can interfere with our time together?' Then shut your mouth. And if you're sitting down when you ask that, even better."

I paused to let Debbie absorb what I just said.

"It's only natural that you love and want to help your father, Debbie," I said gently. "But a man like Mike who shows up consistently for nearly three decades wants to hear that he's a good man some of the time. But he'll only know you see him that way when you put him above all others, your father included."

Debbie wiped a tear with her handkerchief. She looked at Mike, but couldn't find any words to say.

"I want you to cherish me like you do him," Mike said like an astute student.

It warms my heart hearing my clients ask for what they deeply desire in real time.

"I'm sorry," Debbie said, tears coming down her face. "I'm so sorry I didn't show you that."

It was time to take the win.

"We've covered a lot here for today," I said. "Can I leave you something to think about before we wrap up? It won't take but a minute for me to explain."

"Sure," Debbie said, giving me permission.

"When two people are contemplating the future of their relationship, they always end up at the same place: questioning if their commitment is strong enough to keep them together."

"One thing's clear to me," I continued. "There is more here than just pain. A lot more."

Debbie smiled at Mike as she picked up her purse.

"This hasn't been an easy one," I said, acknowledging Debbie's tears. "Can I give you two vows to think about this week?"

"Sure," Debbie said.

"I don't expect you to make them just because you like my face," I said to soften what I was about to ask them to do.

"Oh, we don't, so you won't have to worry about that," Mike said, jokingly.

"Beautiful—that means these vows can stand on their own," I laughed. "Seriously, though, here's what I'm hoping you'll say to each other: 'I commit to holding your well-being ahead of my own. And, I commit to showing up better today than I did yesterday.'"

"Wow, not asking for much, are you Jonathan?" Debbie objected.

"I've worked with enough couples to know this," I began, "You don't have to know how to do either of those things very well. But if you want joy back in this relationship, there's no avoiding making them."

I repeated the vows for them, and stood up.

"Do those vows sound like something you could consider?"

"I think we can do that," Debbie said, answering for them both.

And with that, they stood up, too.

Once again, Mike helped Debbie with her coat and started for the door. Only this time, her arm was tucked under his.

Let's Pause Here...

I've been staring at an empty lot beside my house, wanting to build a Bali-inspired, two-bedroom guest house for the last four years.

And at the start of every dry season, I ask myself, "Is this the year I'm going to start?"

Four years of dreams. Four years of no guest house.

That's my reminder that you can't get what you want without action.

Forgiveness works the same.

No amount of asking for it will get it. And while we all need to learn how to give it freely, consistent effort makes it a lot easier for your spouse to open that door.

Odds are, if your partner's angry and sad, it's because they don't feel chosen by you.

So how do you fix that? By asking:

"What's one small thing I can do today to show you that I choose you?"

That question is more for you than it is for them.

Because it's a mindset. And a personal call to action.

And if you want to take that one step further and get them seeing you as a soulmate instead of a roommate, remember these two vows:

- I vow to hold your well-being ahead of my own.
- I vow to show up better today in our marriage than I did yesterday.

These vows have the power to define a marriage. They push resentment out, and open the door to forgiveness. Your relationship changes when bitterness is replaced by tenderness.

But that only happens when you make these two vows your mission.

You made important vows on your wedding day. But when you live these two vows every day, your partner feels chosen—every day.

One last tip, since I'm on a roll. At this critical point in your healing process, you don't want to ask, "Why do you want to leave?"

That question forces them to rehearse the reasons as to why they should. You don't want that any more than I want to go to the dentist.

Instead, frame your curiosity for their lived experience differently.

Ask questions that show you're ready to lead and act.

Questions like:

1. *"When did you stop feeling chosen by me?"*
2. *"What pain have I caused and never fully repaired?"*
3. *"How can I show up better—and what does that look like?"*

It may hurt to hear some of their answers.

But whatever you do, pay attention to what they say like your marriage depends on it.

Because it does.

Chapter 14

Don't *Try* Harder (*Be* the Person They Fell in Love with Again)

It had been two weeks since our last session. Debbie had left me a voicemail saying there'd been a medical emergency and they had to cancel it.

Judging by what he was wearing, I could tell something was off with Mike. He usually showed up to our sessions wearing an embroidered button-down from work. But today, he had on an oversized hoodie that made him look like a teenager from the 90s.

"Sorry for the last-minute cancellation," he offered as they sat down.

"Of course, don't mention it. Is everything okay?"

Debbie took over, "Mike had a stroke last week."

"Oh my God! Are you alright?" I looked at him. "How are you here today?"

"I'm fine. 100%. Never felt better," he answered with pride.

I couldn't tell if he was telling the truth or not.

"We caught it early." Debbie patted Mike's knee, like the confident nurse she is.

"Thank God," I said. "Does that mean the prognosis is good?"

"Yes. Very good." she replied calmly. "He's almost back to normal."

"Well, that's good. How did it happen?" I immediately regretted asking. A good therapist doesn't pry into the details of a client's life. As minor as this misstep is, I can do better. I made a note to bring that up with Susan in supervision.

"He was sitting on the edge of the bed, trying to put on his socks. All of the sudden, he started slurring his words. I knew immediately what was happening."

"Wow, I'm so glad you were home," I said. "And that you're a nurse, too."

"So am I," Mike smiled at Debbie. "If it wasn't for Debbie, I wouldn't be here right now."

"That's almost certain," she added. "But I'm not sure if I can stop it from happening again in the future. He's back to eating hamburgers. Against doctor's orders, of course."

"Hey, I'm working on it. One thing at a time. First us, then I'll get to my diet."

I liked that. The humor, that is. Nothing is more reassuring than a couple joking with one another.

"Let's keep going then—but only if you're sure."

"A little stroke ain't going to keep me down," he said, putting me at ease. "I've also got some good news."

"Oh, what's that?"

"Debbie committed to your vows. Well, partially at least," he beamed. "I had to show up after that."

"Wow, that's exciting!" I said, making a note to find out what partial meant.

"I admire how you didn't quit, Mike. That shows a lot of commitment."

"It's Debbie you should be admiring," he deflected. "She actually came to me and said she'd agree to them before the stroke happened."

"Well, that's even more inspiring."

"I'd say," he agreed. "I'm not sure I'd have bounced back as quickly without that. If she's willing to work on us, I'm gonna keep on fighting!"

"Does that mean we can talk about the elephant in the room?"

"Depends on which one you're referring to," he replied.

"Good point," I said. "So, until now, I'd tabled the Adam situation in my mind."

"Oh, that's all taken care of," Debbie interjected.

Mike nodded to Debbie, "Tell him what you told me."

"Oh, it's nothing earth-shattering," she began, downplaying Adam's role in why we're here. "I simply thanked him for being a good friend. For lending his ear and all that. And told him, 'Mike needs me now.'"

I certainly wasn't expecting to hear that so soon. But Debbie was no nurse by accident. She was an expert at triage and knew when to act before a crisis got worse.

"Well, that's one down," I said, checking off my to-do list. "Moving on: are you ready to talk about intimacy?"

"Depends how fast you're planning to move, Mister," Debbie flung at me. "Just because Mike here goes and has a stroke on me doesn't mean I'm jumping back into bed with him."

"Don't worry," Mike laughed. "I'm not sure it'd work right anyway."

Nice. We're still keeping things light.

"I hear you. We'll go slow," I said, reassuringly. "I'll do my best to not kick the beehive."

"I appreciate that," she affirmed. "Stroke or not, I'm not going easy on him."

Mike took Debbie's hand. "I wouldn't expect you to. I didn't go easy on you."

"Good one, Mike," I said, acknowledging him.

"I'll take whatever she wants to throw at me," He looked at me and said. "I deserve it."

Mike was giving Debbie permission to throw the kitchen sink at him, so I decided to turn the heat up.

"I love that we're off to a good start," I said, relaxing a little. "But there's something I need to check."

"Go ahead," Debbie signaled her willingness.

"What did you make of those vows I gave you in our last session? Particularly the part about holding each other's emotional well-being ahead of your own?"

I glanced at Mike briefly before settling on Debbie.

"You up for that?" I asked her.

"I have to be honest with you, Jonathan…"

Uh-oh, I thought. That doesn't sit well with her, like so many of my other clients.

"I struggle with the idea of putting Mike's needs ahead of my own."

"I get a lot of pushback on that one, Debbie."

"As you should," she fired back at me.

"Gimme a little leeway," I said confidently. "I think I can convince you."

Debbie cracked a frown.

"Try then. But I can't promise you anything."

"I can accept that," I said. "Back to the task at hand. First, I didn't say 'needs.' I said 'well-being.' Those are radically different things."

I let her absorb that.

"Only one of those words actually creates connection. Can you tell which?"

"I sure can," Mike chimed in. "We know it's not the word 'needs.' That kills it. Makes the hair on the back of your neck stand up."

"That's exactly what it does," I said, smiling at him. "That's why I use the word 'well-being.' It doesn't feel like an obligation—it makes you want to do it, because you're on the same team."

Debbie looked confused. Or irritated. Perhaps both.

"How so?" she asked.

"Because you're both after the same thing," I said. "You both want to be well, right?"

Debbie nodded slowly.

"If Mike makes your well-being his top priority and invites you to do the same, doesn't that feel like something you could say yes to? Wouldn't that feel like a real marriage?"

"I suppose so," she answered.

"You do you, I do me...that doesn't sound like much fun, does it?"

"No, not really." She still looked unsure. "So, I guess I can agree to not say 'needs.' But I'm still confused why his well-being should come before mine. Explain it to me like I'm five."

"Look, you guys are parents," I leaned forward. "I know Justin did stuff to upset you. But no matter what he said or did, you still put him first, right?"

"That's right...we never stopped," Debbie said.

"Putting his well-being ahead of your own?" I said, finishing her thought.

Debbie didn't say anything.

"You didn't say to him, 'because you hurt me, I'm going to stop showing up for you.' Am I wrong?"

Debbie's shoulders dropped. "Putting it that way, you're not."

"So you've been putting the well-being of someone you love ahead of your own for the better part of two decades."

"It still feels like I'll lose myself if all I do is take care of him," Debbie said softly. "Wouldn't anyone feel that way?"

"Of course they would," I said. "But remember, I didn't say 'taking care of him.' I said, 'putting his well-being ahead of your own.' There's actually a difference. But look…you've carried a lot in this marriage. That's not lost on me. Mike's anger. The drinking."

I looked at Mike. He sat there in silence. No defensiveness.

His heart was finally catching up to what he'd been ignoring for years.

"You didn't deserve that, Debbie," I continued. "And none of this will land unless Mike acknowledges what he's put you through."

Mike sat up.

"I know what I did," he started to say. "I made our home a place where she couldn't relax."

Nice. Mike is showing up.

"I'm glad to hear that you understand that," I said to him.

"So how can I let her know that I don't want her to lose herself anymore?"

"Well, that's a great question," I said, with no intention of answering right away.

I looked at Debbie.

"Debbie, I'd never come out and ask you to forgive Mike for the big hurts," I said to her slowly. "You'd have no capacity to if I did. It'd be far too soon to even suggest that. But, would you have any bandwidth to think about the smaller hurts you could forgive?"

"I suppose I could start small," she said.

"Good," I said, acknowledging her willingness. "Even a small start would be a big step. Micro-hurts cause damage over time, and they feel…"

"Like death by a thousand cuts," Debbie blurted out. "That's why it's hard to be in the same room with him."

"I completely understand that. And I'm sure Mike understands that, too."

"I can feel the cold shoulder these days," he acknowledged. "It's hard to miss now."

"If those hurts don't get dealt with, they'll build over time," I said. "You've got 26 years of history and, in that time, there's been a lot of hurt coming from both sides. That turned to resentment, and resentment nearly ended this marriage."

"I can't argue with you there," Debbie said.

"So let's deal with them. Let me give you something to think about."

I looked at them.

"Are you open to hearing it?" I asked.

"By all means," Mike bowed in his chair.

He's liking where all this is going. And so he should. I'm basically going to ask Debbie to forgive him for years of poor behavior—albeit slowly.

"This question is about the future, about the marriage you want," I added. "And it's meant to get you both using your creativity and imagination. Are you ready for that?"

"Maybe," Debbie said.

"Not giving me much, but that's okay," I said, shrugging off her hesitation.

"Just let him ask," Mike said, jumping to my aid. "Before you close your mind."

I could have hugged him at that moment.

"Thanks, Mike. Here goes," I said. "I want you guys to ask yourselves: 'how would our relationship change if we kicked resentment out of it?'"

I looked at Mike.

"Resentment doesn't belong here anymore than alcohol."

Then I turned to Debbie. "Or Adam."

"Both of you can decide right here, right now, to kick it out," I said, challenging them. "You can still be angry when you're hurt, but you don't have to catalog it."

They sat in silence, taking it in.

"I've been married 17 years. One thing I've learned is that being upset doesn't mean you have to walk around with anger or bitterness. That's what lingers after the hurt. And as long as you carry both, it'll be hard to be a good partner to one another."

"This marriage won't survive if we don't do something about this," Mike said.

"It most certainly won't," I said, agreeing with him. "Listen, if we can't let go of the hurts and the resentment, then there's no hope in putting each other's well-being ahead of your own. Your relationship will feel like a competition of two people looking out for their own best interests, instead of looking out for their shared interests. That's what makes a relationship feel unsafe."

"I can see that," Debbie said, signaling a small shift.

"Those two vows I gave you last session are a commitment to show up for each other and the relationship. And they're a commitment that pain and resentment can't survive."

Debbie and Mike locked eyes like two first-graders on the playground made to shake hands after a shoving match.

"Now that I've explained why any of us would want to make those vows, do you feel a little better about making them?"

"I do," Mike said.

Of course you do, Mike, I thought.

"I do, too," Debbie added. "But only as long as he sticks to them. I'm not going to play the doormat again if he wakes up one morning and reverts to his old self."

"Mike hasn't missed a single word," I said. "I've no doubt he's committed to this."

I turned to him.

"You're not going to prove me wrong now, are you?" I asked, knowing his answer.

"Look, I've no idea how much time I've got left," he began, "but with what time I do have, I want to be a better husband to my wife."

"Good," I said, looking at Debbie.

"I think we can move on now, to the hardest part," I said with a grin.

"What's that?" Mike asked.

"Forgiveness. There's a lot of it waiting for you. Could you guys be ready for that?"

And with that, I shut my mouth.

Forgiveness is a choice only they can make.

If they don't make it, they won't own it.

Debbie gave Mike a small smile and then turned to me.

"I might be open to that," she said. "But if we don't know how, what options do we have?"

"Good question, honey," Mike added. "We definitely need help with that."

"I'm glad you asked," I said, reassuringly. "Just because you don't know how to do something doesn't mean it can't be done."

"Okay," he said.

"I'm going to be honest with you," I said. "I've no clue what unlocks forgiveness. If I had it, I'd give it to you. And I don't know when it will happen. But I do know this: it'll only happen if you create the conditions for it."

"Are you saying we have to want to forgive before we learn how?" Mike asked.

"That's exactly what I'm saying."

Debbie was tapping her fingers against her knee.

"I'm being way more vague than I mean to be," I said, looking at Debbie. "Do yourselves a favor: kick the question of 'how do we forgive each other' down the road until you've got some positive momentum happening."

"How do we do that?" Mike asked. "Get some momentum, that is."

"In three ways, Mike," I answered him. "First, stop rehashing old wounds and start expressing your wants."

"And that works because?" Mike again.

"Because you can't solve your problems when you're in pain. But when you help each other get what you want, you will. Does that make sense?"

"Yes, it does," Mike answered.

"Second, separate your partner from their actions. They can do something you don't like, but if you label them 'bad' for doing it, you paint them in a corner they can never get out of. 'You hurt me, and therefore you must be bad.' Can you see the harm in that?"

Debbie's tapping stopped. I must be connecting with her, I thought.

"Third, when your partner asks for what they want, your reply is simple: 'How can I help you get that?'"

You could heal an untold amount of relationships if you could just get people to understand that resentment is caused by starving a relationship of the give and take it survives on.

And once that starvation begins, the doom loop of despair takes over. The second one partner feels like they're getting the short end of the stick, they stop putting in—especially emotionally. Then, you've got two people waiting on the other to go first.

That's how resentment feeds itself and blocks forgiveness in the process. You can't forgive someone while looking at them with a side-eye.

So whether you're reading this with your partner, or alone, practice this question: *how can I help you get what you want?*

I don't care which one of you goes first. The reality is that you both have to go first, just at different times.

Get good at asking that question, and your partner will soften. Stay consistent, and they'll start asking you the same.

I took a sip of water.

"That's how you do it. Three ways to create the conditions for forgiveness: express your wants, separate your partner's behavior from their identity, and help them get what they want. What do you think?"

"That makes a lot of sense," Mike said to Debbie. "Can we try that?"

"I'm willing to give it a shot."

"Mike, I've got one last thing for you."

"Hit me with it," Mike said.

"You've been seeing paper tigers as real tigers for a long time. And it's shaped how you treated Debbie for a long time."

"And Debbie," I said, looking in her direction. "Intended or not, many of your choices have made Mike feel like the black sheep."

Debbie nodded.

"We don't need to dig into all the ways you guys hurt one another over the years, but I will say this: if you can talk for hours about what the other did to hurt you, you can do the opposite. You should be able to watch the highlight reel of the good here, no?"

"I suppose we could try that," Debbie agreed.

"Wonderful. I'm glad that the cup of coffee I had this morning is working."

"Cup? I'd have guessed you drank the whole pot," Mike joked.

"Touché," I laughed.

"Now, let's get serious," I said. "Time to go after the big win and find the key that's going to unlock your intimacy."

"You're not going to say we have to start cuddling and touching more, are you?" Debbie asked with a look of concern.

"Absolutely not. We're going to take it slow—let the connection take its course."

"Good. I'm not sure I'd be ready for that."

"And nor should you be," I said, reassuring her again. "But what if we took the approach of stacking wins?"

"Stacking wins?" Mike repeated.

"Yes. Like the pro golfers do. When you're teeing off on the first hole, you've no idea how to get to six under par. But if you take it hole by hole, before you know it, you'll be putting on the green jacket at the Masters."

"Debbie, what do you think?" Mike said quietly.

Debbie smiled. "It makes sense. If we take it slow."

"Here's the thing, Debbie. You don't even need to worry about taking anything slow. Because we're letting intimacy develop just like a child learns to crawl."

"In what way?" she asked.

"You raised a son, so this should be easy to understand. Kids need to crawl before they can walk, correct?"

"Yes."

"Well, that's not quite accurate. They need to hold their head up with their neck first. Then prop themselves up like a cobra, then crawl, and then walk. And I've probably missed five more milestones. I'm not a parenting expert, as my wife likes to remind me."

They both laughed.

"Back to stacking those wins. Let's close this session with some low-friction homework."

"Sounds good," Mike said. "I like homework: it gives me something to do."

"Great, then you'll like this," I said. "Back when you were dating, before things got serious, what did you do to fall in love?"

"Well, we went for a lot of walks. And ate a lot of ice cream," Mike said, smiling.

"Anything else?"

Debbie smiled at Mike and said, "Don't forget camping! And those notes you used to leave under my windshield wiper," she added.

"Love that!" I said. "So lots of walks, ice cream, camping, and letters."

"Yes, that's right," Debbie said.

"Did you notice that? In less than a minute, we've come up with a bunch of different ways to take you back to where you fell in love. Now, when was the last time you did any of those things?"

"Been a really long time," Mike confessed.

"None of that sounds hard to do," I said, looking at Debbie. "I wonder, what do you think would happen if you did a little more of that again?"

Mike sat up a little straighter and looked at Debbie, "Doesn't sound hard to me."

I nodded. "Right?"

I could feel Debbie's guard coming down.

"No, you're right. I think I could do that," she said.

"I love it," I said, my smile stretching ear to ear.

"Thanks, Jonathan," Mike started to say.

"Woah—one last thing before you go. I promise. Just a simple conversation starter to bring you a little more connection, if you're ready for it."

"Okay, Jonathan," Debbie said. "But don't press your luck. You've been asking a lot today."

"I know, I know," I grinned. "What can I say—I'm tenacious."

She laughed.

"Today, I've asked you to put down your resentments and lean into forgiveness. Now I'm asking you to be curious."

"You really better wrap this up, Jonathan," Mike laughed. "I'm starting to wonder if you're the one who had the stroke and can't stop talking."

That one nearly sent coffee shooting out of my nose.

"But seriously, though," I continued. "If you want safety here, you have to start with curiosity."

"What are we talking about then?" Debbie asked.

"Nothing complicated," I answered. "Just ask each other: '*What's one* want *that you feel good about asking for?*'"

"Is that it?" Mike asked, looking surprised.

"That's it," I said. "Ask it daily, weekly, monthly—whatever cadence feels right. Just be consistent. You don't want to bodycheck them, so try not to get defensive when you hear their answer. And remember, the best reply is that question I taught you. What was it again?"

"How can I help you get that?" they answered in unison.

"Exactly!" I said, smiling. "And that question right there signals you're open to repair. Can you try that?"

"For sure," Mike said.

"I'm willing to as well," Debbie agreed.

"Wonderful. Give that a try this week. Remember, simple requests only—nothing sexual. Imagine you're dating again. You're each other's source of safety and connection. Your only goal is to help each other get what you want. And when the other asks you, you remind them they're in a safe place."

And with that, I closed my notebook.

As they both stood up to leave, Debbie smiled again, "Thank you for today, Jonathan."

"Yes, thank you," Mike echoed.

"I should be thanking you," I said. "Just remember, forgiveness doesn't happen just because you want it."

I paused for effect.

"But if you're willing to look for it, you may just find it."

Let's Pause Here...

My wife and I have a strong marriage. But it didn't always feel that way.

We've had a strong connection from the moment we laid eyes on each other. But my anger wanted to sabotage that.

My wife deserved a man who could treat her well. Too often I showed up as the boy who couldn't.

Still, something kept her connected to me. And it had little to do with attachment styles or love languages.

It had everything to do with finding the man inside me that she fell in love with.

So how do you find that man inside of you?

It's not by looking at the man in the mirror. It's by looking at the man behind the eyes.

Every single one of us is wounded in some way.

That's as true for Mike and Debbie as it is for me—and likely you.

Becoming the version of yourself your spouse fell in love with doesn't mean getting a glow-up, hitting the gym, or eating better.

They want you to strip away the behaviors that made them dislike you in the first place.

You have to go back to being the person who won them over in the beginning. Back to the time when being better or trying harder came naturally.

And it came naturally because you wanted them. Because you chose them.

So choose them again.

And the best way to do that is by asking who you were when they first chose you:

"What parts of me did you fall in love with?"

But don't stop there. You need as much detail as you can get. Follow up with:

"What made you say yes to our second date?"
"When did you know I was the person you wanted to spend the rest of your life with?"
"What did you see in me that maybe even I couldn't?"

If you pay attention, they'll tell you who you were when connecting with you came naturally.

After you've both gone deep, here's how forgiveness happens:

1. Stop rehashing old wounds. Give each other the space to express what you both want.
2. Separate the person from their behavior. Your partner is good even when they make poor choices.

3. There's a magic script that can soften even the hardest shell: *"How can I help you get what you want?"*

I know perfectly well that everything I've asked you to do here will be hard for you to remember—especially when you're in pain.

But if you can sprinkle even a few of these questions into your daily interactions, like I have, you'll have a smile on your face knowing that the hill of forgiveness you have to climb is nothing compared to your buddy who didn't read this book.

Chapter 15

No Time Like Now (You Don't Get Back the Moments You Miss)

Two more weeks had gone by since I last saw Debbie and Mike. Thankfully, no further medical issues kept them away, just busy schedules.

As Mike walked into my office, I noticed a small skip in his step.

"You're looking happy today," I said.

That kind of positivity is usually a good sign. It means something has shifted.

"I've been looking forward to this," he said.

"I guess there's a first time for everything," I joked. "Must be the new coffee I switched to."

"Don't be a smartass," he said, laughing.

Mike feels comfortable calling me that, and I'm glad. It means we still have rapport.

"Don't keep me waiting. After our last session, I'd love to hear some good news."

"I'll let Debbie tell you," he said. "I'm not taking credit for this one."

Debbie had taken her seat, almost unnoticed.

"Hi, Debbie. Good to see you!" I said. "Mike's smile distracted me for a moment."

"Relax," she said. "We didn't have sex, if that's what you're thinking."

"No, of course not," I back-pedaled. "What's the good news then?"

"It's not as big a deal as he's making it out to be."

"Then it shouldn't take but a second to give me all the details."

Debbie was still giving off a cooler vibe than Mike. But a shift had clearly taken place. She wasn't clutching her purse. She'd set it down on the floor.

"It's been a good couple of weeks. Mike's been trying really hard."

Good, I thought. He's taking the assignment seriously.

"Yesterday, I got in my car to go to work, and there was a note under my windshield wiper. I was briefly annoyed that I had to get back out, but it was sweet. He asked if I wanted to go for ice cream."

"Ah, like the old days?"

"Yes, only this time I could barely read it," she said, fighting a frown.

"Ahh, I get it. We do so much on our computers, our handwriting has gone to crap," I said.

"I wish that were the case," Mike said.

"It was hard to read...because of the tremors," she said, dabbing her eyes with a Kleenex. "From the stroke."

"Doctor said it can be a delayed symptom," Mike said, with a slight shake in his voice.

"They can sometimes appear a month or so after the initial stroke," Debbie said. "In 90% of cases, it resolves on its own. But it could require medication—or worse, surgery. We won't know for a while."

Debbie reached over and put her hand on his. I hadn't seen her do that before.

I had the sudden urge to cry.

That was a shift. A small one, but profound. Like the first crack of sun coming through your window at dawn.

It wasn't tears of joy that I was holding back. It was tears of sadness. It had suddenly hit me that I never saw my parents touch each other like that my entire life.

It's one thing to witness conflict, but to see actual repair like the kind Debbie and Mike were doing right in front of me, made me think of their son.

How proud would Justin be to know his parents were fighting so hard to save their marriage?

I sat there for a moment. I didn't want to ruin it. Every small win needs a witness. And this small moment told me something very important: there is still air left in this relationship.

"Look at me," Mike's voice cracked. "I'm shaking like a mess."

He looked at Debbie and started to cry.

"Not much of a man to be proud of these days."

"I am proud of you," Debbie squeezed his hand. "I haven't liked you for quite some time, but you've always been there for our family."

"I feel like a failure and disappointment. Like I was never enough."

"I've never said that," Debbie said. "I've always thought you were selfless. Passionate—for better or worse—but selfless."

"Thank you for saying that," Mike smiled. "I don't think I've ever heard you say that, to be honest." He paused for a moment, and then tentatively added, "Can I ask you something?"

"Me, or him?" Debbie asked.

"You," he said.

"Of course. That's why we're here."

"Why was it so easy to shut me out? Why did it seem so effortless to always make it about him?" Mike asked, obviously referring to her dad.

Debbie looked stunned, but her defensiveness was gone.

"You always chose him. It was always, 'My dad needs me for something....'"

Mike struggled to catch his breath. I could see a little sweat dripping at his temples and started to worry that it might be too much for him.

"Are you okay, Mike? You sure this isn't too much?" I checked in.

"I'm fine. Just the blood pressure pills," he said to reassure me.

I had instant flashbacks of my dad. After my father's stroke, he couldn't climb a flight of stairs without needing a towel waiting at the top to dry himself off.

"This is a touchy subject," he continued. "That's why I'm working really hard to take our conversations down a notch or two."

"Well, you've been doing a great job at it," Debbie injected.

"I appreciate that," he smiled. "I'm trying to lead with vulnerability... not pain, like the good doc here's been saying."

"Not a doc, Mike. Just saying," I chuckled.

"I'm just pulling your leg."

"Go on," Debbie encouraged him. "I want to hear this."

"I want to show you that I can be upset with you and at the same time keep it contained. So this is just as much about your need for safety as mine."

"I appreciate that."

"I've had to swallow a lot of pride, to admit that I've screwed up. That I've hurt you."

Keep going, Mike, this is good, I thought.

"And made you feel unsafe. And I'm okay with that," he paused for a moment. "I mean...not what I did. Just saying that."

"Thanks for clarifying that," Debbie said with a laugh.

"But I want you to acknowledge your part in this. Just a little. What you did to get us here."

Mike looked at the floor.

"I need to know it's not just me that wants our family back. That you're choosing me. Choosing us."

"I've got to hand it to you, Mike. How you said that was beautiful," I said, then instantly regretted stealing Debbie's moment to respond. I tried to bring it back to her.

"If I can point out one thing," I began, "While you shared that, Debbie kept her hand on yours the entire time."

"She must be trusting me again," he replied.

"Exactly," I smiled.

"Debbie, did that feel better to you?"

"It did," she confirmed. "A lot better. Like we can actually talk without the emotional blowback."

"That's gotta feel safe," I said. "Safe as in, how he's saying it."

"It does," she confirmed. "And I can speak to what he said, if I may."

"Of course. Please do," I encouraged her.

"I felt pushed away. The drinking. Your stress. It was exhausting."

"And then I had my dad to take care of. Not just now—always. Ever since my mother died."

Debbie looked at me as if to make sure I was still listening.

"I grew up worrying about my father. So saying no to him…especially now that he's sick…I didn't think I had it in me."

"And the thought of two men mad at me—I just couldn't handle that."

Her voice cracked when she said that.

"But you were loyal to him since way before I came into your life."

Debbie paused for a moment.

"You're right," she admitted. "And I'm sorry. He always made me feel like it was my obligation."

"That's really hard," I said softly.

"I should have shut it down after we got married. I should have paid more attention to how my relationship with him affected you. And how he treated you."

"I needed to hear that," Mike said, smiling again. "I've felt alone for a very long time."

I scanned their faces.

"Since no one's looking for the exit anymore, let's close some more distance," I said.

They're finally communicating from a place of safety. That's worth building on. At this point in the session, I needed to pause the hard talk and switch gears.

Why?

Because pain doesn't disappear from relationships. And only a fool thinks talking about it until they're blue in the face helps.

It doesn't—it sends sessions sideways.

Debbie and Mike need to take the win and downshift. If it took 26 years to reach this level of emotional decay in their marriage, a few weeks of therapy isn't going to get them out of it completely. But if we pause the pain, we can build on this positive momentum and get to work exploring what a stronger connection could look like.

And I'm going to do that by debriefing the assignment I gave them last session.

"Can we circle back to what I asked you to do last session? You know, the part about helping each other feel good about asking for what you want? I'd love to hear where that took you."

"That went better than expected, actually," Mike started.

"Oh, please tell," I replied.

"The other day, I worked up the courage to ask Debbie if we could stay off our phones for the evening."

"Nice, Mike!" I said. "Now that's what I'm talking about."

"Oh, it wasn't that hard, to be honest," he replied. "It's been bothering me ever since Steve Jobs released the first iPhone."

"Hey, it's not that bad!" Debbie quipped. "But he's right, I'm on my phone too much. My dad, Justin, they message a lot."

Sounds like my wife, I couldn't help but think. I can get a lawyer's attention easier than hers with everything she does to run our family and businesses.

"And? Did that go over well? How did the evening go then?"

"Amazing. We put the phones away and made it through an entire movie without interruptions."

Mike beamed.

"I've always hated watching stuff with her when her phone's beside her. It feels really disconnected."

"I like that," I said. "And I couldn't agree with you more."

Time to bring Debbie into the conversation. I looked at her.

"Did that move the needle at all for you, Debbie?" I asked.

I'm trying to orchestrate this moment of connection. I want them to note this little step forward and store it as a memory. It's evidence. Evidence that with action and effort, change is not just possible, it's inevitable.

"For sure. And it was nice," said Debbie, looking at Mike.

"It was more than nice. It was great, actually. We had more conversations than ever before," Mike added. "We held hands."

"Oh, wow! That must have felt good," I said with enthusiasm.

"It did," Mike said. "It felt like we were just hanging out. Like two people who actually wanted to spend time together."

"Can we stop using that word 'actually,' already?" Debbie sounded slightly irritated. "I like spending time with you, when it's Big Mike I'm spending time with. But when it's Big Dread...ah, no thanks."

"I hear that."

He put his hand on his chest and looked at Debbie, not letting go of her hand.

"You need to know something. Big Dread is dead. He ain't coming back. The stroke took him out. It's just me left."

"If you'd said that a month ago, I'd never have believed you."

Debbie locked eyes with Mike.

"Does that mean you're giving us a chance?"

"Well, if by telling my dad I can't fill his prescriptions this weekend, then yes," she said proudly. "I think you can assume that I'm giving us a chance."

I don't think I'd ever seen such a large grin on a grown man's face before. It made him look like Big Mike had been body-swapped for his 16-year-old self.

I wasn't about to waste my chance at tackling the only thing remaining: their lack of intimacy.

Two years. Those words still hung on the wall like a big neon sign. Debbie and Mike hadn't been intimate that entire time. And although our sessions were filled with progress, I hadn't brought it front and center like I normally would.

And with good reason. Their pain and resentment had made that impossible.

But Debbie was softening. And Mike was growing. If now wasn't the time to broach the subject, I didn't know when would be better.

"I think it's time we talked about something," I said.

"Uh-oh," Mike was the first to respond. "You make it sound like we're in trouble or something."

"Not trouble," I began. "But we haven't fully talked through the intimacy part."

Debbie's shoulders tensed.

"Don't worry," I said gently. "No one's going to be asked to do something they're not ready for."

Go slow, I told myself.

"The biggest problem when intimacy is missing in a relationship is the message it sends."

I looked at Debbie.

"That could be that I don't feel safe with you."

I turned to Mike.

"Or that there's something wrong with me."

"Well, that's a true statement if I ever heard one," Mike said, nearly shouting. "I put her through the ringer!"

I respected his ownership.

"That's accurate, Mike," I said, agreeing with him. "But not completely. There was something wrong with your behavior, yes. But as a man? You're a good man: loyal, faithful, honest, and committed. That counts for something, no?"

"Well...yeah, I suppose," he said.

The trouble with blaming the person for why physical connection dies is that you're reacting to the "bad" parts of them and ignoring the "good." And that puts you in a tough spot: how good does a person have to be for us to be intimate with them?

Most people don't know the answer to that. And even if they did, what happens when your spouse gets close to being "good" enough—and then slips up? Does that reset the clock and delay repair even longer?

Personally, I believe that asking why someone caused intimacy to die is the wrong approach.

I leaned forward.

"All that matters is what happens from here," I said. "We need to close the distance. Because for a long-term relationship to survive, it needs a healthy intimate connection."

Debbie nodded.

"I know there are lots of reasons intimacy disappears," I continued. "I've got pages of notes filled with them."

Mike let out a little chuckle.

"But we're not focusing on that today. And we're not going to focus on what you're capable of either—be that a hug, a kiss, or anything more."

I paused to set the pace.

"I've got two things for you to think about."

"Like what?" Debbie asked.

"In the early days, intimacy felt natural and you used it to send a message to each other. Do you remember what that message was?"

I answered for them:

"It was, 'I want a relationship with you. I want to feel close to you.' But now, you're in that relationship already. So it's about feeling close again."

I looked at Debbie first.

"What message would it send Mike by letting closeness back in again?" I asked her.

"I guess Mike would feel good knowing I wasn't pushing him away," she said.

"And what message do you want Debbie to get?" I asked Mike.

"That she's safe to let me in?" he said, looking at Debbie.

This is good, I thought. Really good.

"You're exactly right. But that's just the start. There's one more thing you need before anyone can feel safe again."

They both looked at me.

"You have to like each other again."

They didn't respond.

"Intimacy doesn't begin with: 'I want you,'" I continued. "It starts with, 'I like you. I feel safe with you.' And then 'I want you.'"

Debbie raised an eyebrow.

This was the moment I'd been waiting for since our first session. The moment to go deeper.

"I've got something for you," I started. "But you might want to brace yourselves a little."

Debbie swallowed hard.

Mike squeezed her hand.

"I wonder if sometime this week…."

I looked at Debbie.

"You could tell each other what you like about the other."

Debbie let out a relieved laugh.

"You had me going there for a sec, Jonathan," she said. "I wasn't sure how you were going to finish that sentence."

"I'd never ask you to do what you're not ready for," I said. "But I'll gladly push you to ask: 'How can we bring more fondness back into our relationship?'"

"I like that—a lot," Mike said. "That's not a question we ask ourselves enough."

You're not wrong, Mike, I thought.

"And if your mind draws a blank, ask yourself: 'What do I like about my partner that I'd miss if they were gone?' Simple, right?"

I didn't wait for an answer.

"No one knows when or how the connection you want will come back. But you'll find out when you start liking each other again."

"How do I know that?" I smiled. "Because there's a young man named Justin walking around out there."

They both laughed.

I could tell by how much my back was hurting that our time was up.

"Now that you're putting your phones away more often, I'll leave you with a little more homework, if you're up for it."

"Bring it on," Mike said with enthusiasm. "I'd love to make this a habit."

"Good. But a little disclaimer," I said, warning them. "These aren't silver bullets that'll grow a connection like grass in July. They don't have to be. But they are known to lead to hugs, handholding, and even intimacy sometimes."

"We'll see about that."

Thanks for setting me straight, Debbie, I wanted to say. I chose to side-step her dig instead.

I needed to get them feeling good about their past. If they look in the rearview mirror and see success, they'll have hope that the view out the front windshield will be the same.

Every relationship starts with high hopes. Mostly because it's new, and fresh.

But then it ages, grows colder, and suddenly there's more distance than anyone would care to measure.

Of course, it's up to you to decide if you let yours stay that way, or not.

Me? I'm not letting the fairy-tale I grew up watching on Disney die.

If you want that, too, then you're going to need hope, and lots of it.

The good news is that you don't have to look further than your past to find it.

I uncrossed my legs.

When you're hanging on the couch, waiting for the next season of your favorite show to drop, here are a few questions I want you to run through:

1. *"What is one dream you had for our relationship when we first fell in love?"*
2. *"What did I do in the beginning that made you fall in love with me?"*
3. *"How do you want the rest of 'till death do us part' to look?"*

These questions aren't complicated, but they're not easy to answer, either. They require a little memory and imagination. And that's the point.

"That's it," I said. "Just three simple questions."

"But good ones," Mike said, seeming to have them memorized already.

Good indeed, I thought to myself.

I looked over at their hands and could see Mike's trembling. Then I checked his collar. Still sweating.

What I saw made me think of my dad again. And how he looked in the hospital the week he died. He was convinced he'd be discharged. That's what he told me when I visited him for the last time. He died two days later.

I looked down at my notepad. I was scribbling. Doing my best to fight back my own tears.

I snapped to and made a note to schedule supervision with Susan for next week. I need to let out a good cry, I thought.

"We better get going, Mister," Debbie stood and held her hand out to Mike.

I nearly jolted out of my seat. She was moving fast. Much faster than Mike.

"I'd like to get home before the sun goes down," she added. "You know I don't like driving at night."

"I know, I know. I'm coming," Mike pushed himself up with a soft laugh. "Thank you, Jonathan. Really, thank you."

"It's been a great session. The pleasure's been mine."

Debbie looked at me. She didn't need to say a thing.

We were both afraid for Mike.

But not for their relationship.

Two months ago, Mike had called me in a panic, desperate to save his marriage. Today, he was just trying to keep up with his wife.

When Debbie steadied Mike with a hand on his elbow, I saw forgiveness on her face.

And from the smile on his, I knew he'd keep earning it.

I closed the door behind them and turned the lights off.

I needed a moment in the dark to collect myself. My girls expect a genuine smile when I walk through our front door.

I'd never lost a client. At least not that I knew of.

I'd also never known a man to fight so hard to save his relationship while his body was starting to betray him.

I didn't know it at the time, but I'd never see that man again.

Let's Pause...

...for the last time.

I'm not a doctor. I can't tell you the physical reasons why intimacy fades.

But I am a couples therapist. And when it comes to the emotional ones, I've got a thing or two to say.

I'm not going to say what's on my professional mind. I'm going to say it like a man who's lived it.

For a good 10 years of my marriage, I was Mike. I was the pursuer. The "high libido" spouse.

But between you and me, I was more than that.

I was an asshole.

That's what anger does to a man. It turns him into someone his wife has no desire to be with.

And when the rejection I deserved came, it wasn't confusing.

It was entirely predictable.

Instead of asking my wife what message she was sending me, I spent years thinking there was something wrong with us.

There was. But it wasn't her libido.

It was me—and the lack of safety I caused her to feel.

It took me 12 years of my life and $50,000 of training to figure out that while safety makes intimacy possible, it's not what brings it back.

Only liking each other does that.

If your partner doesn't like you, they won't be close to you.

And if they can't be close, they won't be intimate.

It's really that simple.

So if you're stuck, and you've done the work to show up in a way that makes your partner feel safe, don't ask for more sex.

Start by looking for the things you like about each other. And find ways to say them.

That'll put some gas in your tank and set you both up for the conversation that needs to happen next:

"What message would it send if we let a little closeness in again?"

My guess is that it would mean: I like you. I feel safe with you. And now...I want you.

Six out of seven mornings a week, I walk into the kitchen and find crumbs from my wife's toast all over the counter.

So why do I smile every time I see her mess?

Because I get to clean it up one more time.

I won't get back the moments I lose to frustration. Or the intimate ones I let frustration ruin.

Nowadays, when shit goes wrong in my life, I ask:

"Is this a real tiger? Or a paper tiger trying to steal my joy, and turn me into an asshole that's not safe to be around?"

The day is going to come when there aren't any crumbs to clean up.

I don't want it to be because I pushed my wife away.

I only want it to come knowing I chose her.

And she chose me back.

Epilogue: To Be Beloved

Most couples think they have more time together than they do.

Unfortunately, Debbie and Mike didn't.

They never got the chance to see how far perseverance could have taken them. After a few weeks of missed sessions, I finally got a call from Debbie. Mike had passed away, she told me. Another stroke. Barely choking back my own tears, I asked her how she was doing. She said to me that, in all the pain his death brought her, she was connected closer to him now than she ever was before they came to see me. In the weeks after our last session, she had never felt more loved in her entire marriage. And she owed that to their decision to put the pain down and pick up each other. They held onto each other's hearts in those few short weeks. Whether it was intuition that told them what was coming or the closeness they felt in those final weeks, she wasn't sure. But the day Mike passed, she felt deep in her heart that the two of them had indeed become one.

Vanessa and Julian reached out a year after we met for our last session. Vanessa announced that she was pregnant again. Julian, hard at work as ever, had changed immensely. The juvenile behavior had long since been replaced by an even greater determination to make the three girls (and soon to be fourth) in his life his sole priority. Trust hadn't been completely restored in their relationship. Vanessa needed to see a few more years of evidence to be convinced that twinges of doubt wouldn't hit her at the slightest trigger. But Julian hadn't let his foot off the gas in reminding her that he'd never make the same mistake again. And that gave meaning to the forgiveness she was feeling coming back into her life.

Jada and Chris came in for a few booster sessions with me six months after our last session. Surprisingly, it was not to talk about their relationship, which was a great sign. They wanted help with Jada's youngest son's adjustment to his new school. I couldn't help but point out to them how encouraging it was to hear that the focus of their relationship had moved from sorting their stuff out to helping their son with his.

"Oh, we can still get into a pretty good fight, Jonathan," Jada offered.

"But there are no plates or threats of divorce thrown around when we do," Chris chimed in.

"You know, that's just fine," I said, reassuring them. "Meredith and I know how to get into a fight just as good as the next couple."

"But it's not how you get into one that matters," I continued. "It's how you get out of it that counts."

It's not by accident that all three of these couples' stories ended in success. Every single one made a decision: to move from fear and doubt to safety and reassurance. They chose to change the message they send each other and became consistent in sending it. When they set down their pain, they signaled that they were ready to go first.

Ask any car salesman in the world how he makes his living, and he'll tell you: "I get people to buy what I want them to buy."

What he won't tell you is how he does that.

But I will.

With questions. He asks lots and lots of questions—until he finds the key that'll unlock your "yes."

That's what Mike did. That's what Julian did. And that's what Jada did.

They all asked a lot of questions. Oh, their partners did, too. But let's be real here for a moment: Jada, Julian, and Mike had a lot of convincing to do if they wanted to keep their marriage going for another day.

When I first met them, all three had one thing in common.

They never asked, "How can I get my partner to believe that our marriage can be better?"

Because they weren't asking themselves that question, they struggled. They struggled to convince their partners that there was still hope. And they struggled to believe it themselves.

When you don't ask the right questions, you don't know where to focus your effort. You misunderstand what your partner wants from you. And it becomes harder to buy the time you need to make the changes they want to see.

Eventually, you lose hope.

Why does that matter? Because without the hope that a better relationship is possible, you won't change.

Much like I didn't change for a long time.

For most of my relationship, I wasn't asking what my wife wanted out of it. I did in the beginning, but as soon as the first hurts started to appear, I let my own fears drown out my curiosity for what she really desired.

And that was a regulated husband who made her feel safe.

That's what questions do.

They make people feel safe. Safe enough to forgive, like Debbie, Chris, and Vanessa did. And safe enough for my wife to change her mind when she was about to pack her bags and move to her parents.

Questions are the only tools we have as therapists to change our clients' minds. That's why asking the right ones is critical.

This book is filled with questions that'll help you change minds—your partner's and your own.

It's up to you to believe that asking them will do just that.

And it's up to me to believe that I've convinced you of that.

Unlike the car salesman who wants to sell you something where you don't know what you're getting into, I'll be honest with you. Asking the right questions will work only if two things are present: authenticity and consistency.

Yes, you actually have to be genuinely interested in what your partner's answers will be. You have to be prepared to act on those answers. And you have to do that consistently—day in, day out.

For a man who has worked with thousands of couples at this point and had to win back the heart and mind of his own spouse, believe me when I tell you that actions do in fact speak louder than words.

Actions work so well in fact that, even today, as my wife wraps up her second full-time job as a homeschooling mom (on top of being my business partner), she never, ever complains that her husband is collapsed on the couch, zoning out on YouTube for a few minutes.

Why the grace?

That could have something to do with how hard I work to remind her that she's good enough.

My wife has brought her own wounds into our relationship, just as I have. But because I have made it my mission to help her repair them, the goodwill I've earned keeps her connected and committed.

That's the power of questions.

The last thing I want to leave you with is this: when you get what you want in your relationship, you will stay. When you see what you want to see, you will stay. When you experience what you want to experience, you will stay.

So many couples, when asked, "What do you think of your relationship?" will describe it from a place of scarcity.

They'll tell you what they're missing. What they "need." Or what's happening that shouldn't be.

But they'll rarely tell you what's working. What feels good. Or what they're happy with.

When I hear them speak from a place of lack, I know they're missing something.

They're missing a message.

A message that they crave to hear. A message that will satisfy their deepest desire.

And what's that message?

It's not simply, "I love you."

It's something far deeper.

It's knowing that you matter.

You are enough.

You are their only plan.

It's knowing that if they could do it all over, they'd choose you again.

In a single word, it's this:

Beloved.

Why's that word so important? Because being beloved is entirely different from being loved.

To be loved is something your spouse *feels* for you. To be beloved is what they *think* of you.

In my mind, that can only mean one thing: they like you.

You see, it's more important to be liked than loved. Because if they like you, they'll feel safe with you.

Safe enough to be close to you.

And safe enough to choose you.

So, if I've convinced you to follow my breadcrumbs, don't wait for your partner to choose you.

You may be waiting a long time.

It's more important that you go first. And ask the right questions.

If you do that, or die trying, odds are great that you'll achieve two very important things.

One: your partner will wake up one day and actually believe themselves when they say,

"I am chosen. And I am cherished."

And two: that bed they wake up in when they say it will have you in it.

Acknowledgments

I want to thank Sam, my acquisitions editor at Wiley. Had he not believed that a content creator like myself could string together more than 2,200 characters, this book would never have been written. For the rest of the team at Wiley—Christine especially—thank you for all of your support in making this possible.

I would also like to thank my writing coach, Sheila. You gave me the confidence I needed to believe that what I write is worth more than just propping up your computer monitor.

At my graduation, my first supervisor, Dr. West, told me that we'd be reading about me one day. Dr. West, I only wish you were still here to read this.

To Louise, my supervisor of nearly a decade, thank you for always being real. I'm forever grateful for the clarity you bring when I can't find it myself.

To my sisters and brothers, as spread across the globe as we may be, knowing you're rooting for me means everything.

My father, despite all his flaws, showed me how to be the man I am today—not by what he did but by what he didn't. Even so, I thank him for sending me the message that's as true for me as everyone in this book: we are all loveable.

I was lucky to have a mother who never gave up on herself and who taught me that you do everything for your kids. Without you teaching me that, I'd never have had the perseverance to finish this book.

I couldn't end this book without acknowledging all my followers: none of this would have been possible if you had simply kept scrolling.

And to all the couples who've ever trusted me with their marriages, you're the reason I do this work.

To Meredith, you never gave up on me and followed me everywhere I took our family. For that, I owe you everything and will spend the rest of my life showing you that. You read every word of this book, edited it, gave me feedback on it, and endured the stressed-out husband who wrote it. You know I couldn't have done this without you—but you deserve to hear that.

Finally, to Charlotte and Aria, being your father is more than one of the greatest joys of my life. It's a spiritual assignment. I get to show you how to find love—the chosen and cherished kind—and teach you how to recognize it when you do.

About the Author

Jonathan Van Viegen is a couples therapist and coach, the creator of the Chosen & Cherished Method, and a husband who has spent 17 years learning how to send his wife the only message he wants her to receive: "I choose you."

For more than a decade, Jonathan has dedicated his clinical practice to inspiring couples to build their own Enlightened Marriage rooted in five pillars: honesty, loyalty, transparency, fidelity, and commitment. His relationship insights have generated more than 100 million views online and continue to resonate with couples around the world.

Jonathan lives in Central America with his wife, Meredith, and their two daughters.

Index